HAL LEONARD
GUITAR METHOD

JAZZ GUITAR SONGS

T0081552

PLAYBACK+
Speed • Pitch • Balance • Loop

To access audio visit:
www.halleonard.com/mylibrary

Enter Code
4332-7986-9404-0077

ISBN 978-1-4234-1777-4

Visit Hal Leonard Online at
www.halleonard.com

Contact Us:
Hal Leonard
7777 West Bluemound Road
Milwaukee, WI 53213
Email: info@halleonard.com

In Europe contact:
Hal Leonard Europe Limited
Distribution Centre, Newmarket Road
Bury St Edmunds, Suffolk, IP33 3YB
Email: info@halleonardeurope.com

In Australia contact:
Hal Leonard Australia Pty. Ltd.
4 Lentara Court
Cheltenham, Victoria, 3192 Australia
Email: info@halleonard.com.au

Bluesette

Words by Norman Gimbel
Music by Jean Thielemans

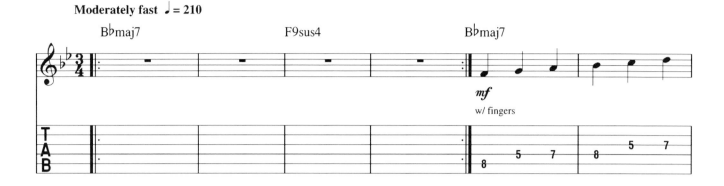

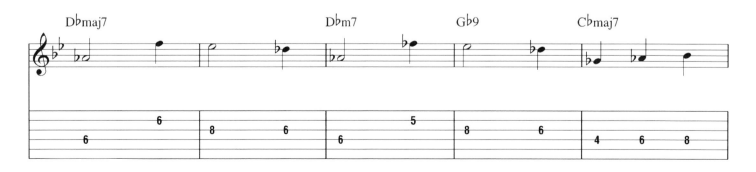

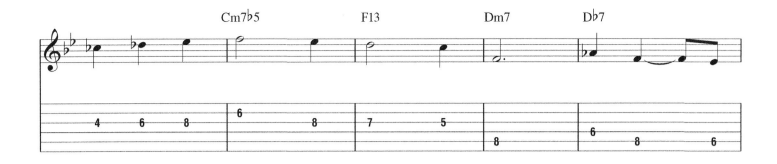

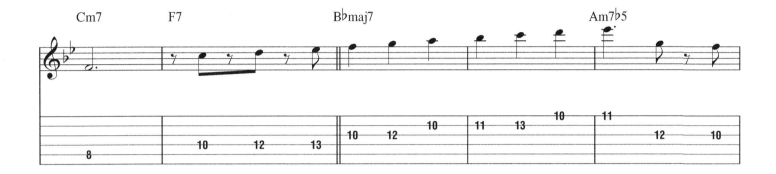

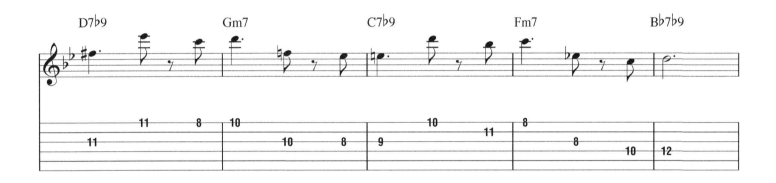

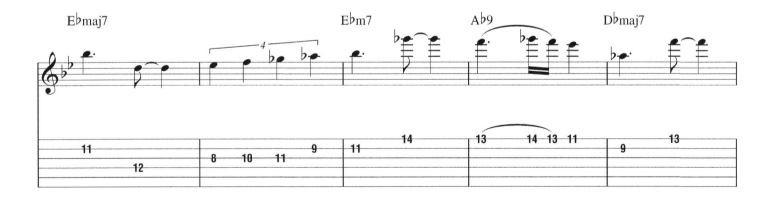

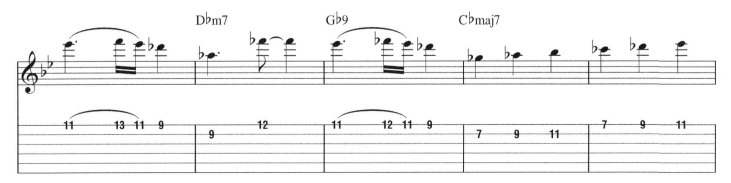

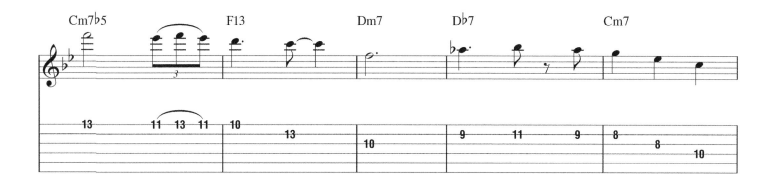

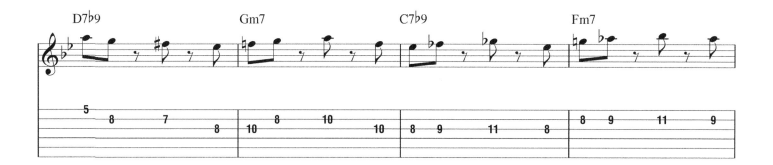

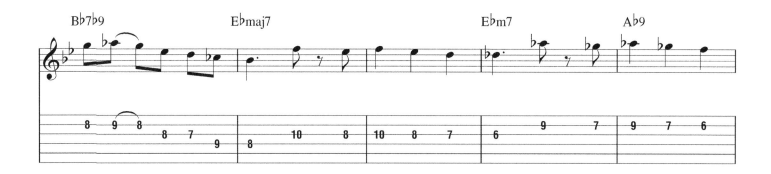

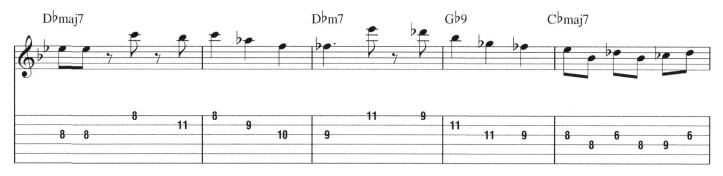

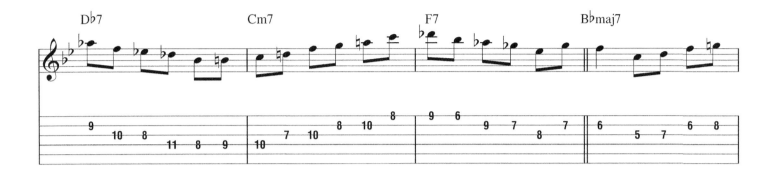

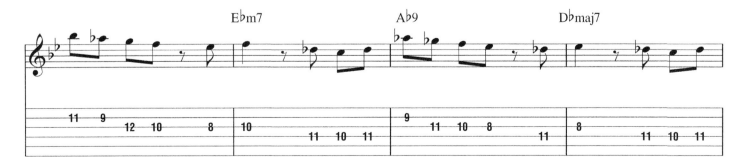

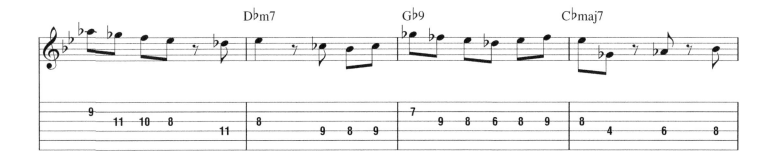

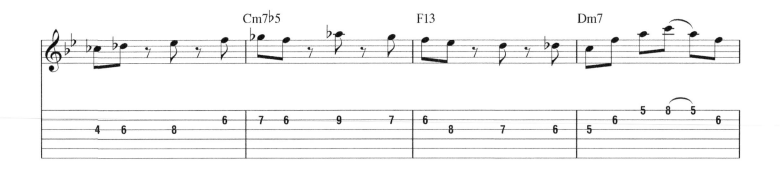

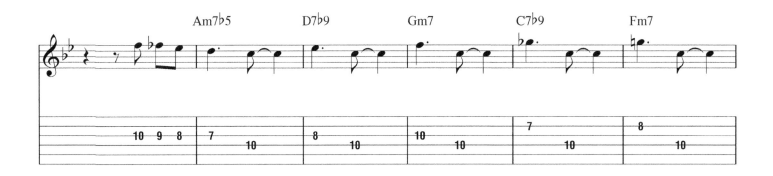

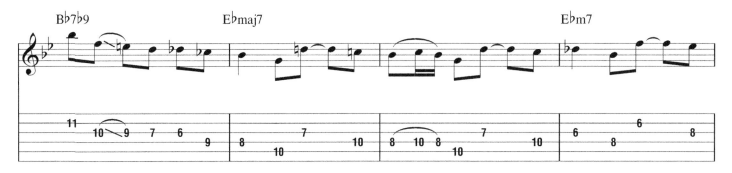

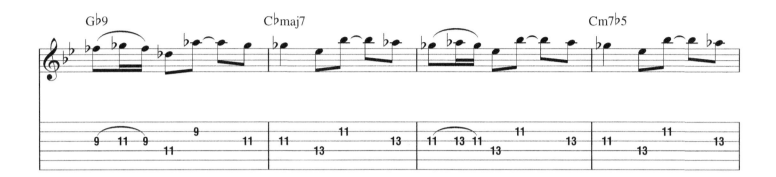

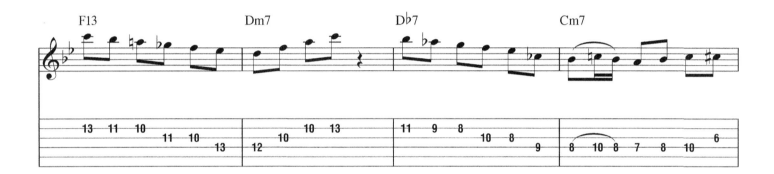

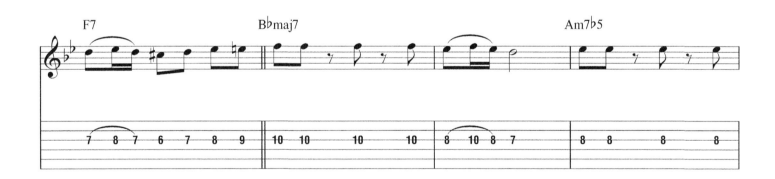

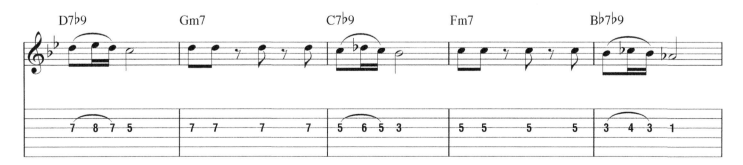

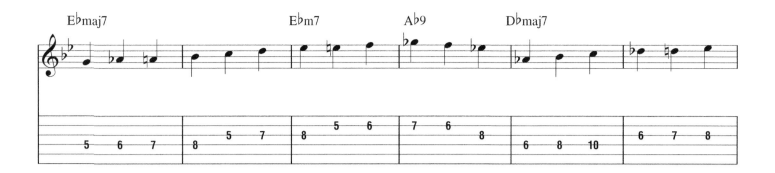

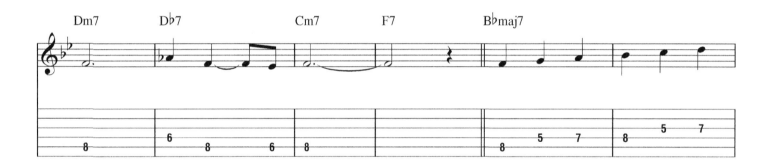

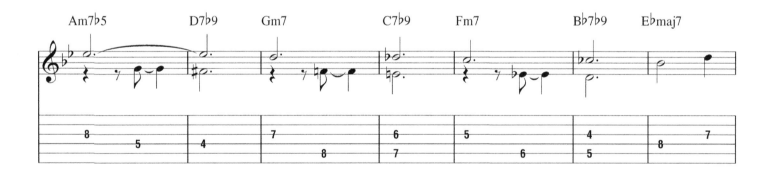

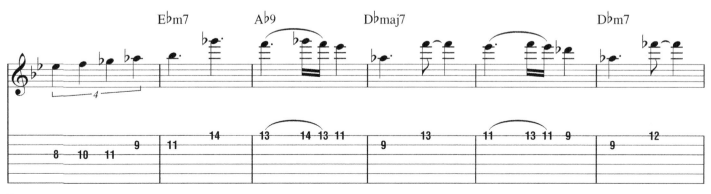

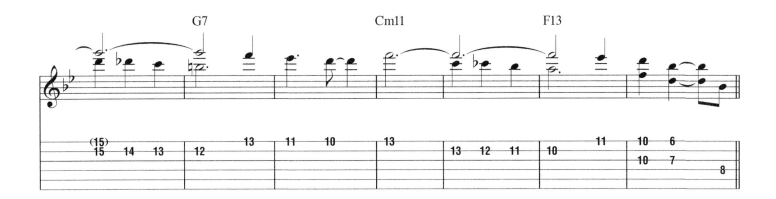

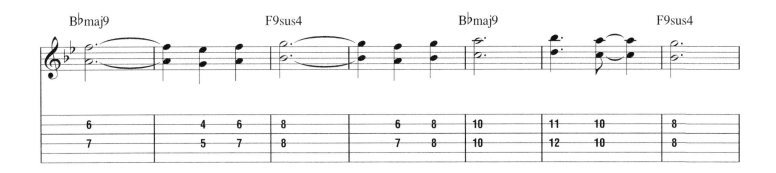

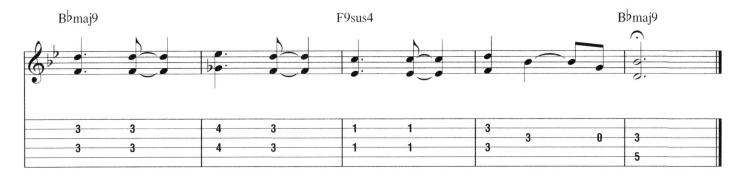

Bye Bye Blackbird

from PETE KELLY'S BLUES

Lyric by Mort Dixon
Music by Ray Henderson

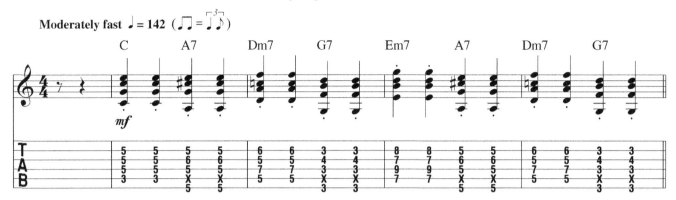

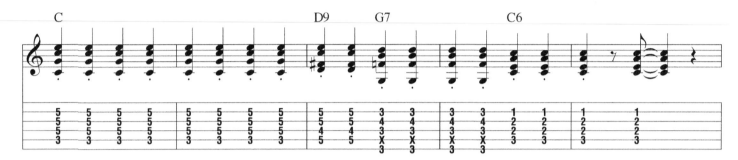

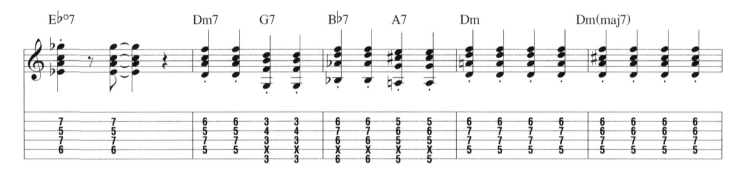

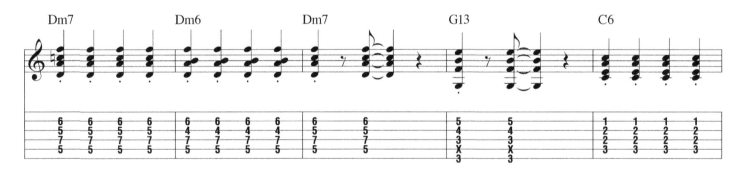

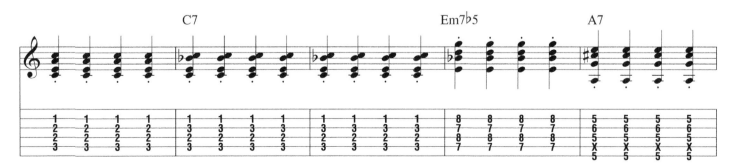

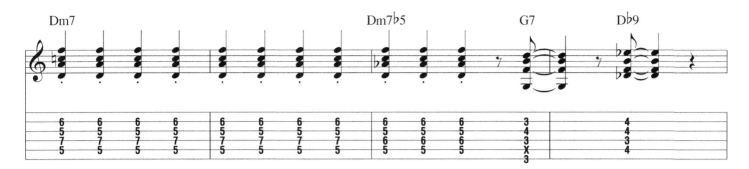

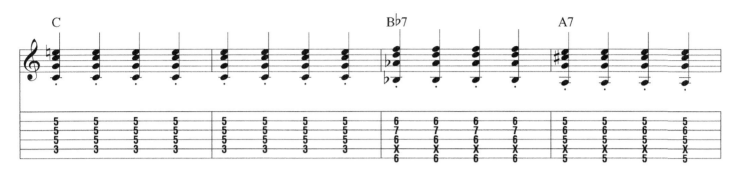

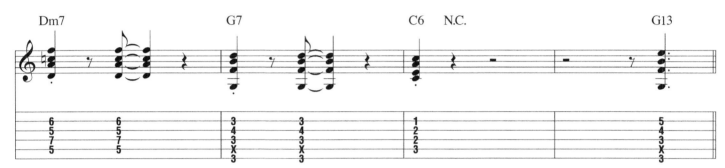

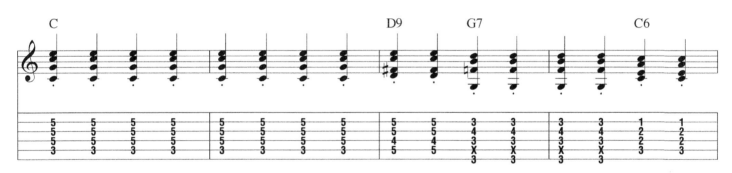

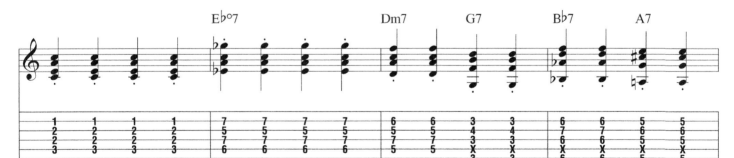

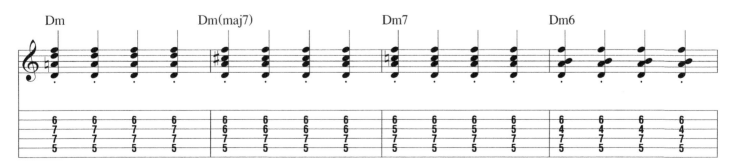

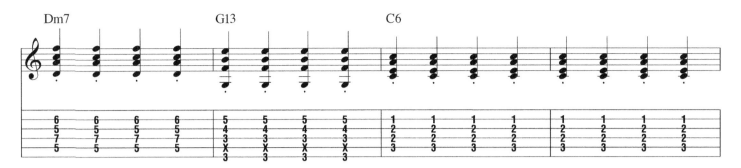

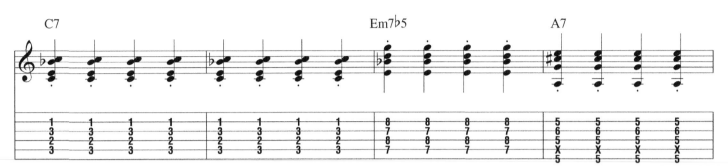

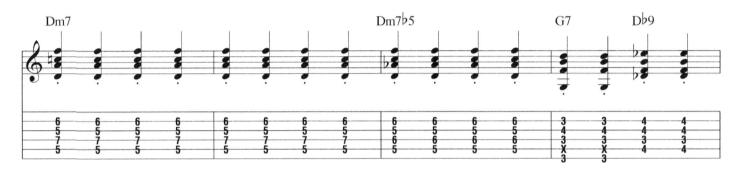

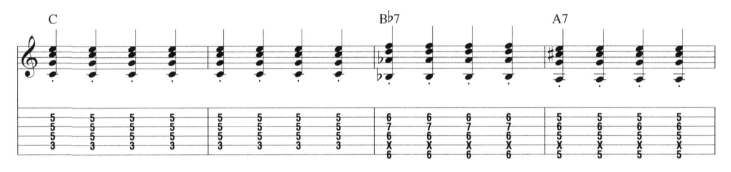

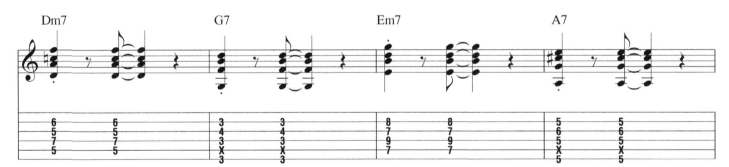

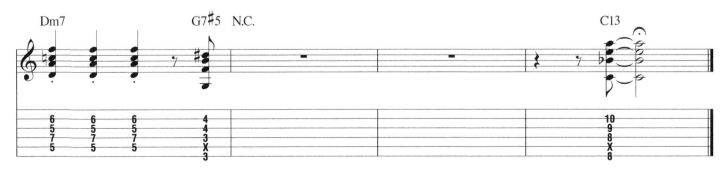

I Remember You

from the Paramount Picture THE FLEET'S IN
Words by Johnny Mercer
Music by Victor Schertzinger

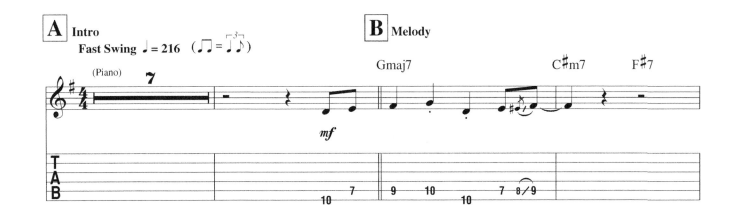

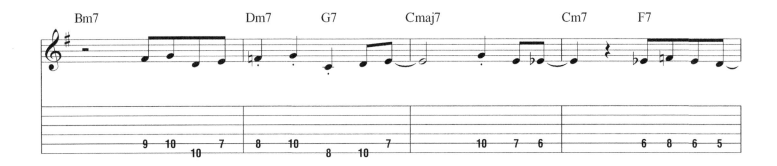

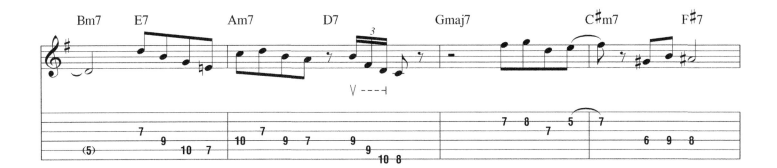

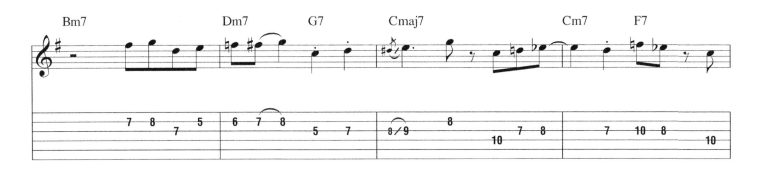

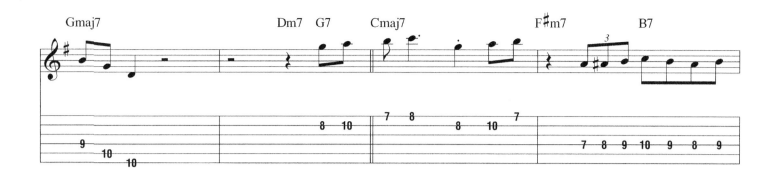

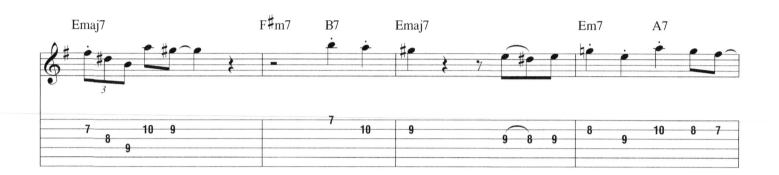

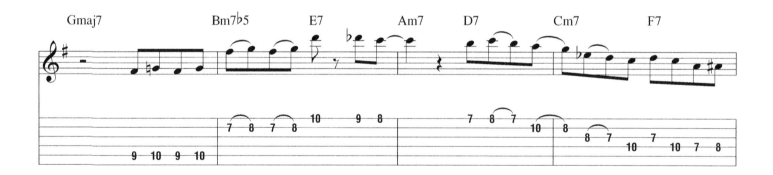

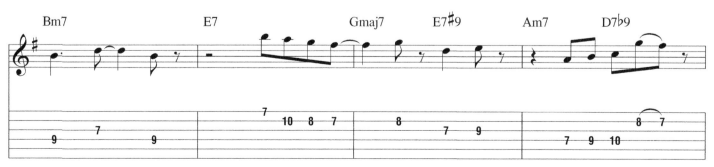

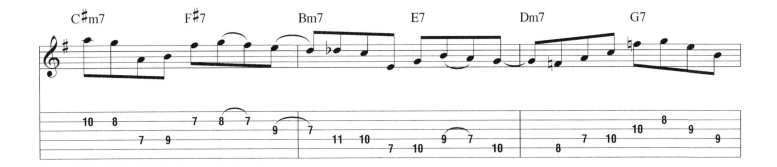

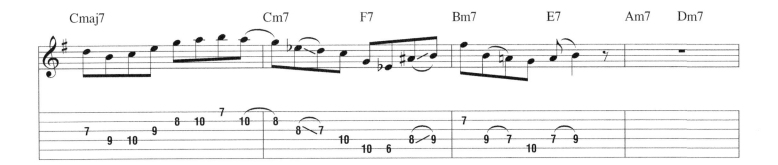

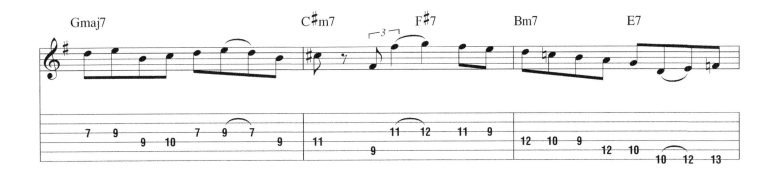

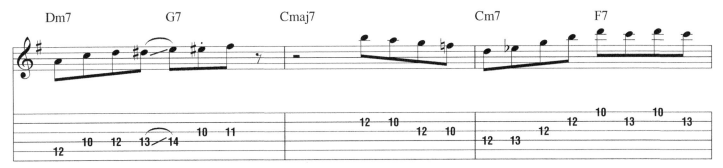

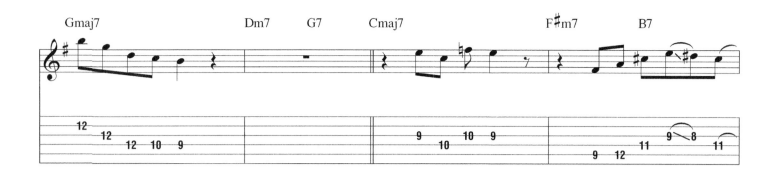

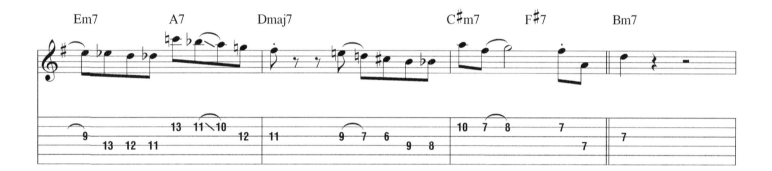

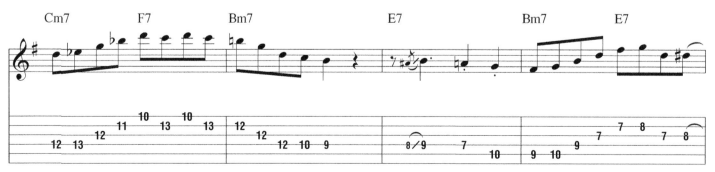

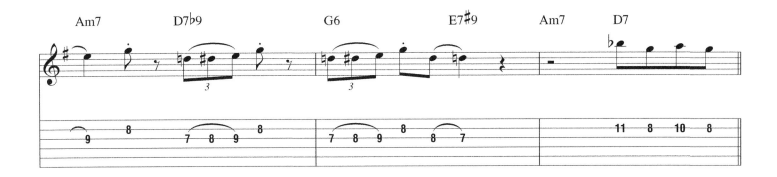

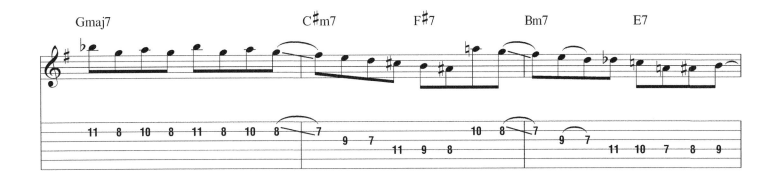

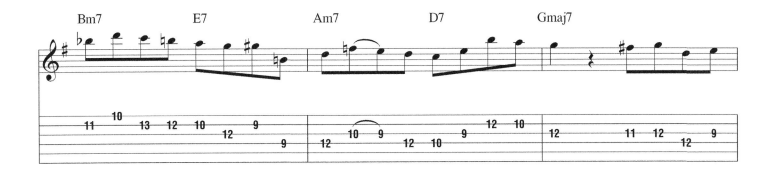

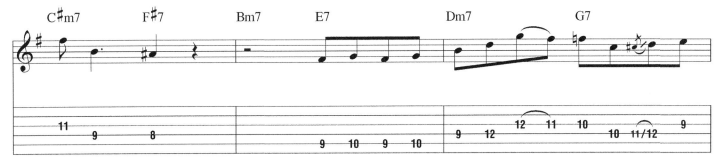

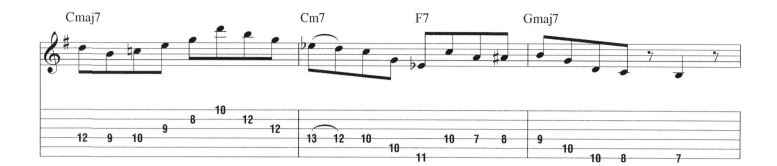

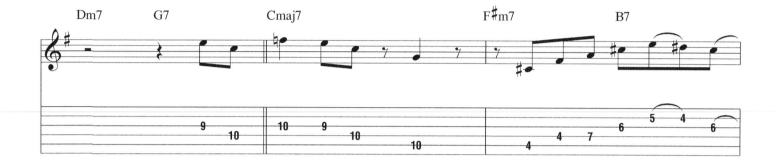

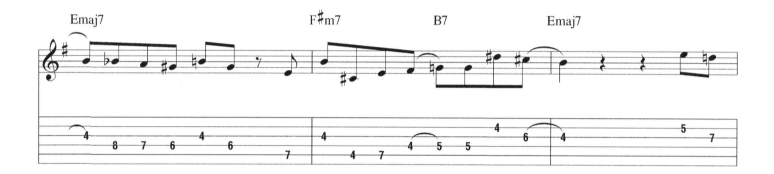

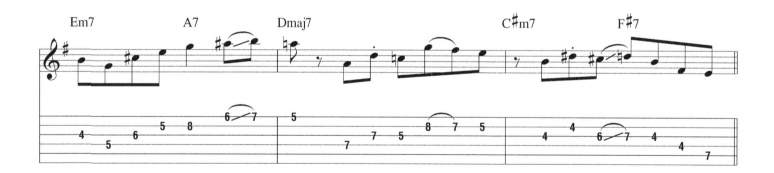

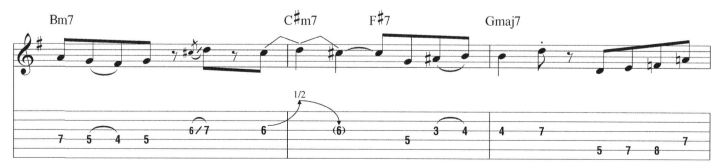

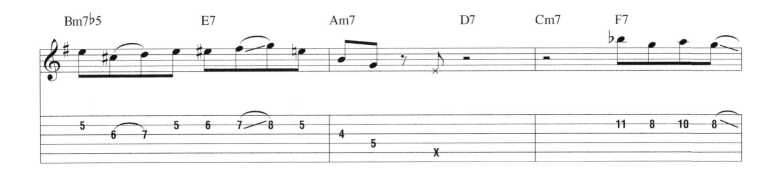

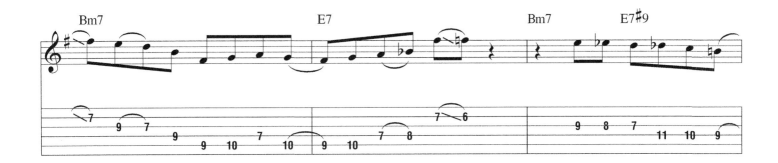

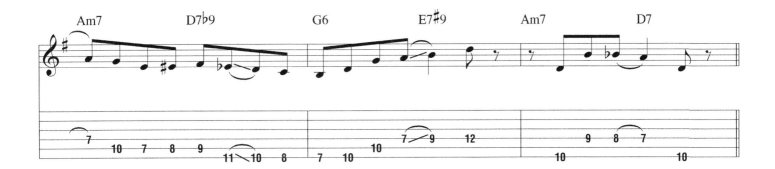

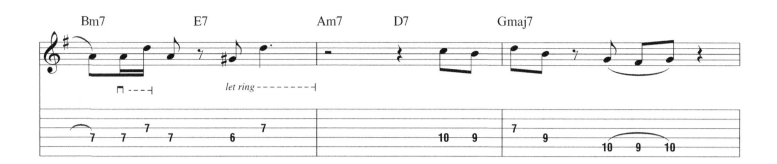

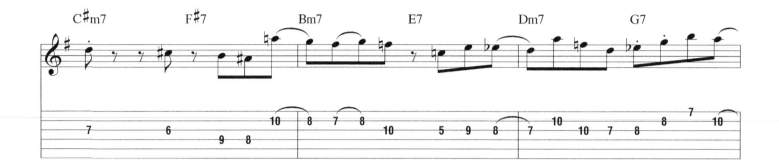

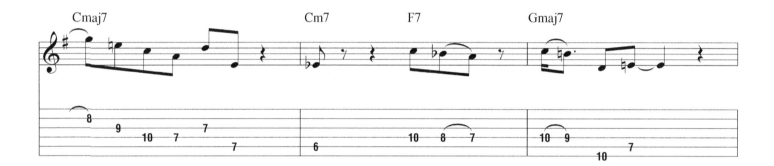

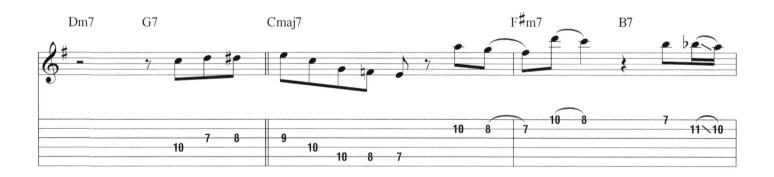

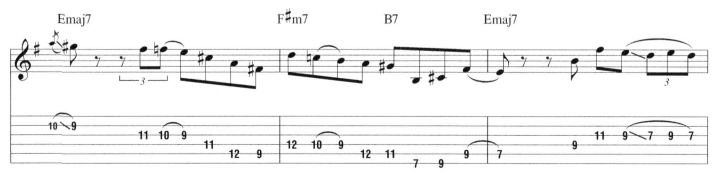

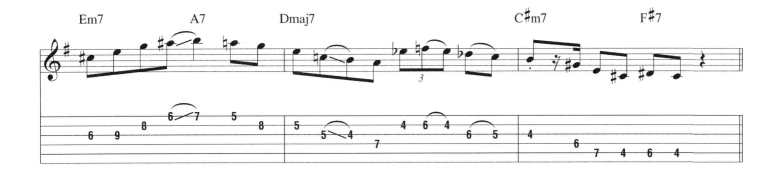

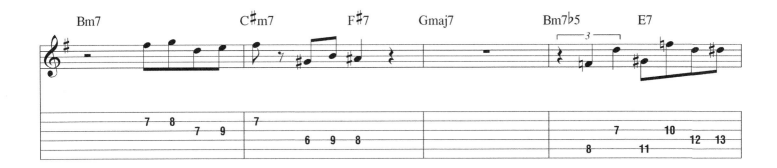

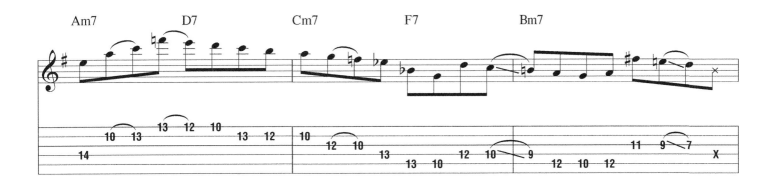

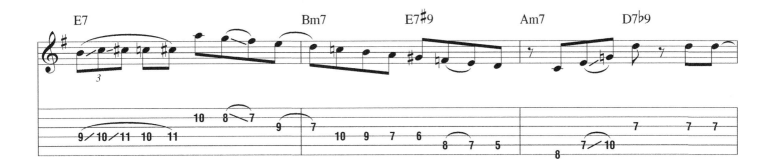

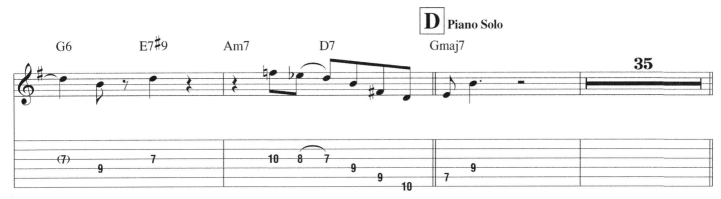

E **Melody**

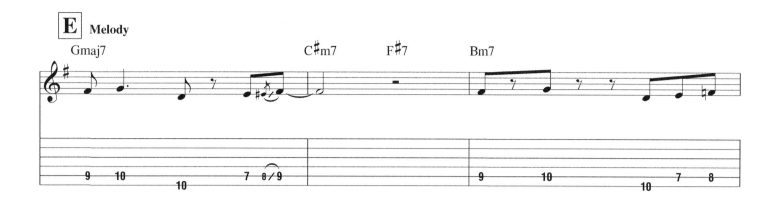

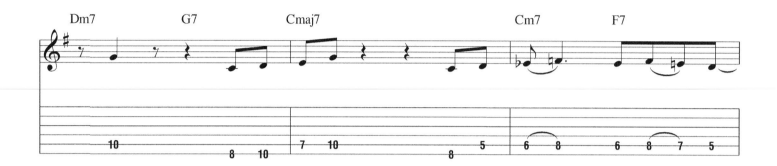

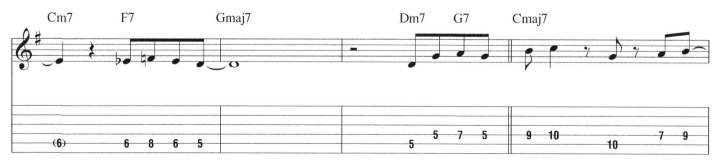

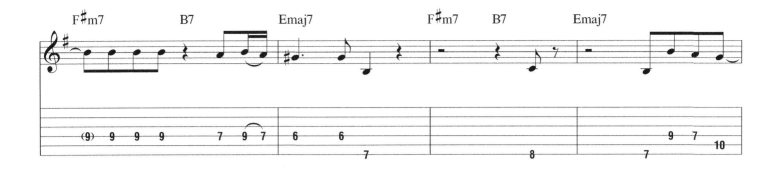

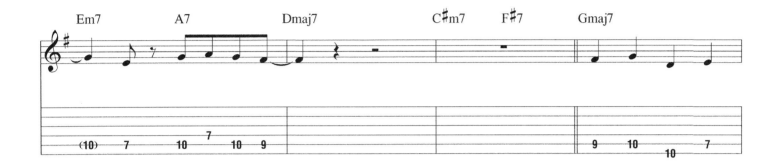

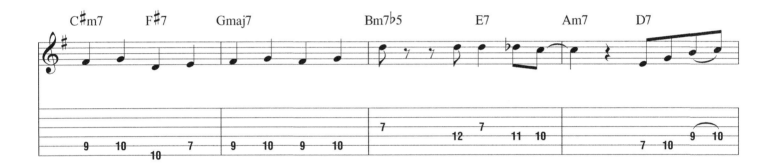

The Girl from Ipanema
(Garôta de Ipanema)

Music by Antonio Carlos Jobim
English Words by Norman Gimbel
Original Words by Vinicius de Moraes

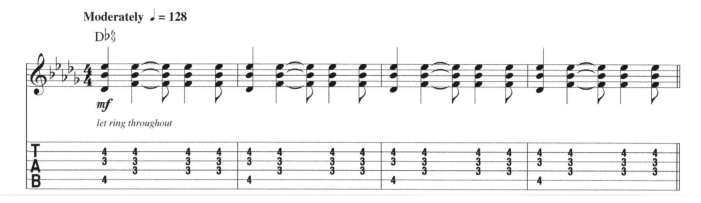

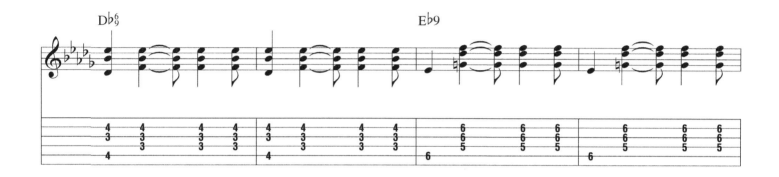

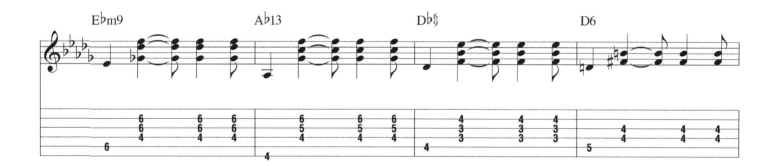

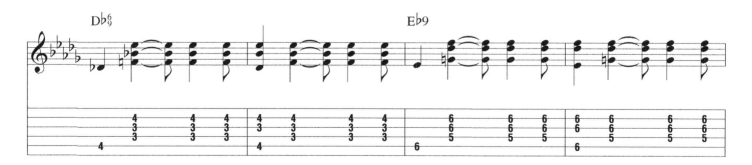

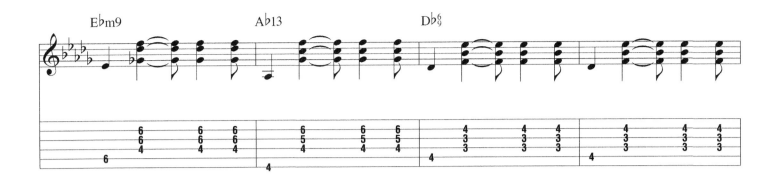

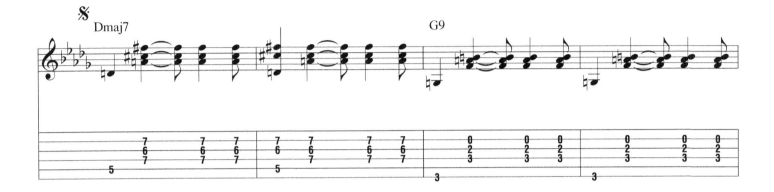

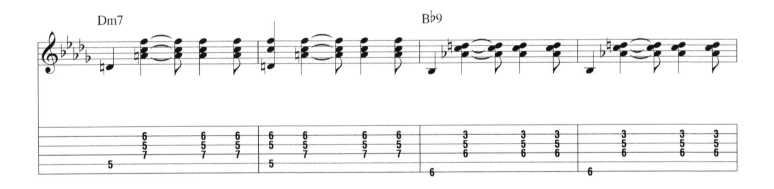

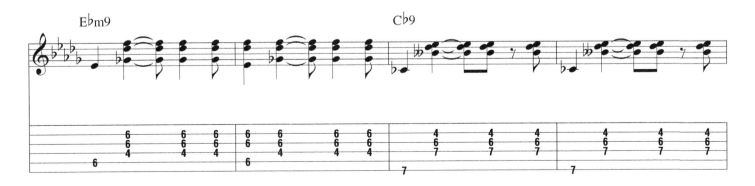

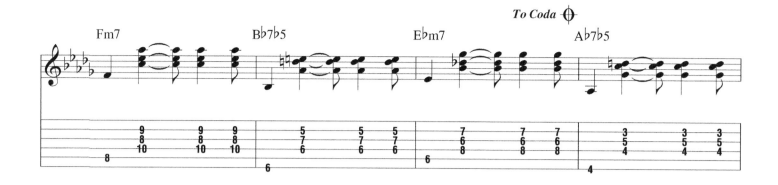

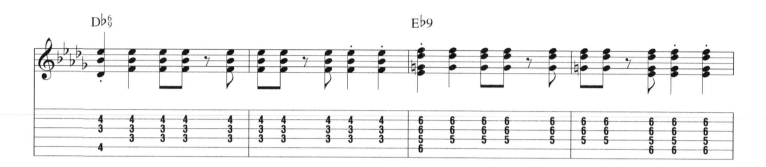

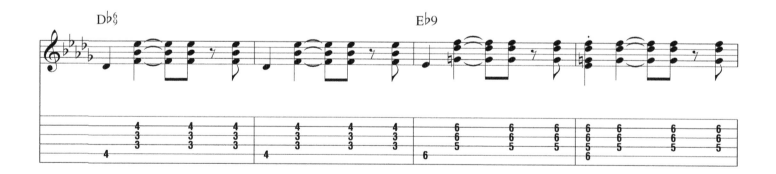

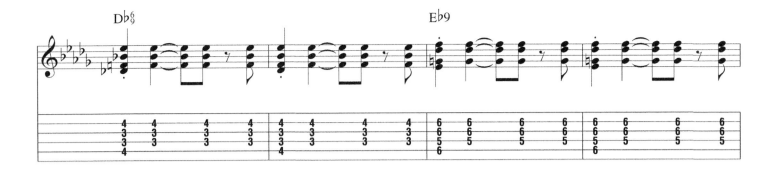

D.S. al Coda

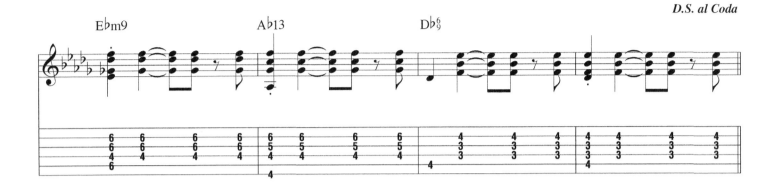

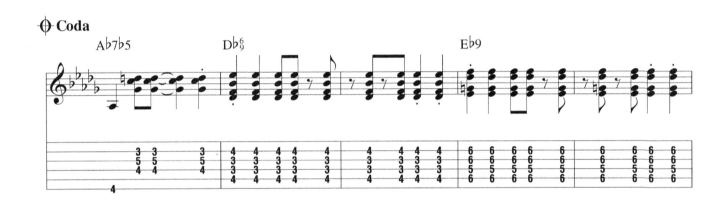

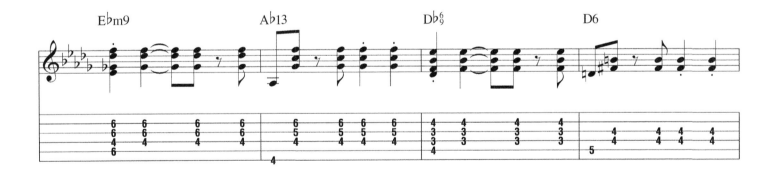

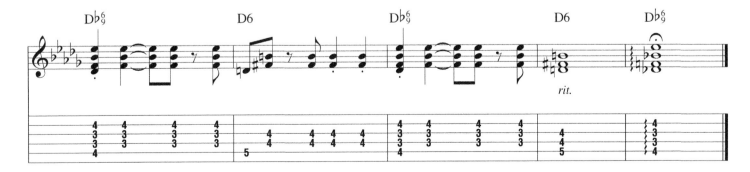

Honeysuckle Rose

from AIN'T MISBEHAVIN'
from TIN PAN ALLEY

Words by Andy Razaf
Music by Thomas "Fats" Waller

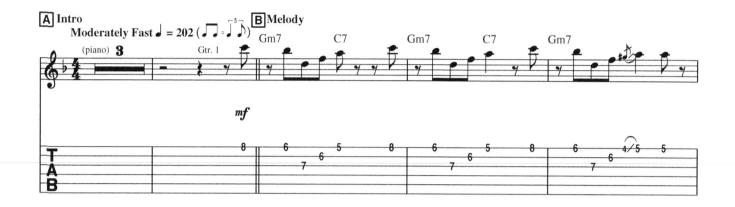

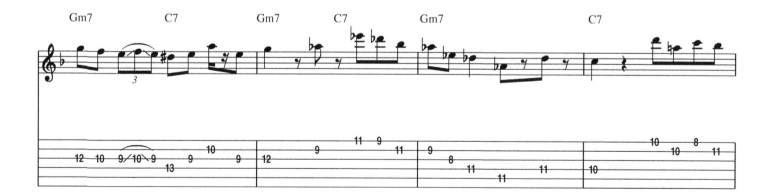

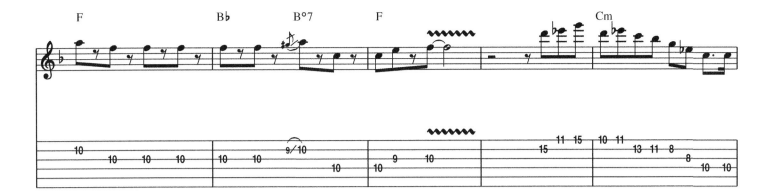

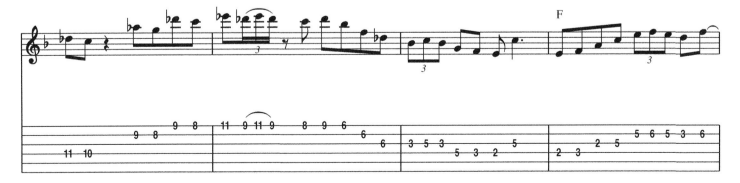

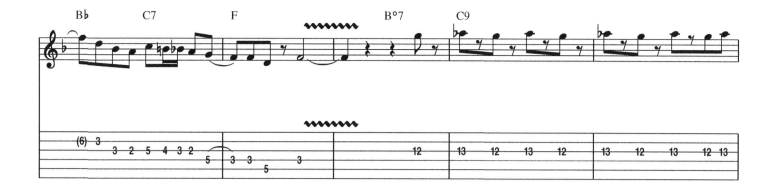

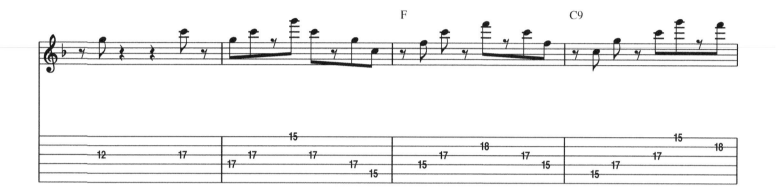

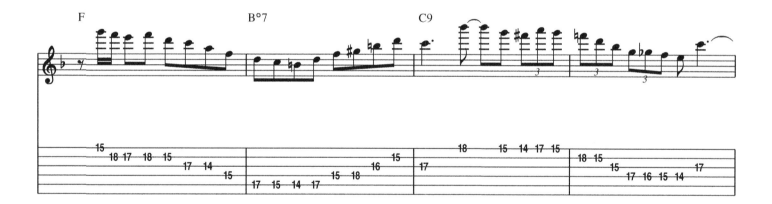

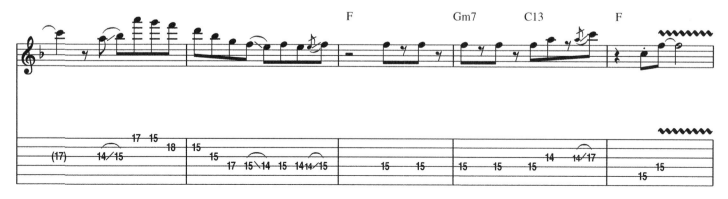

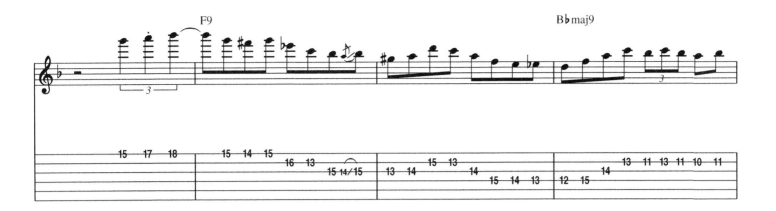

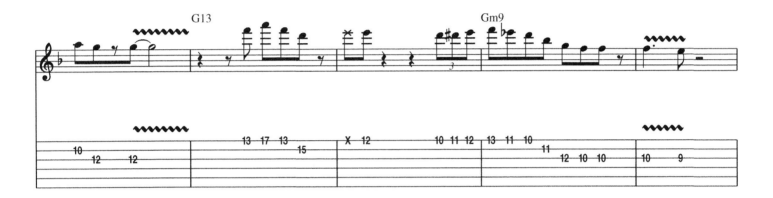

31

D Guitar Solo

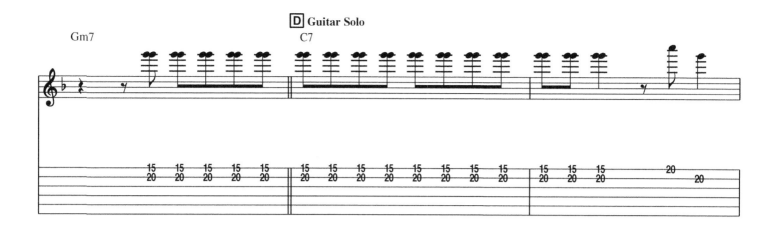

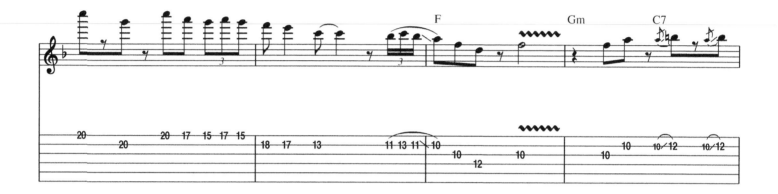

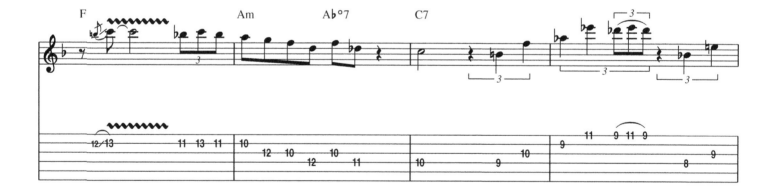

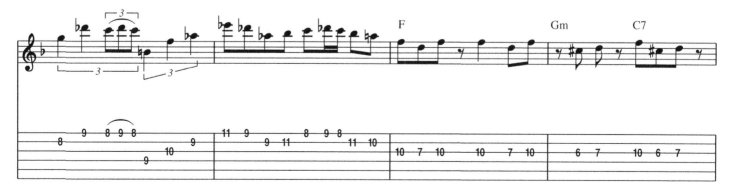

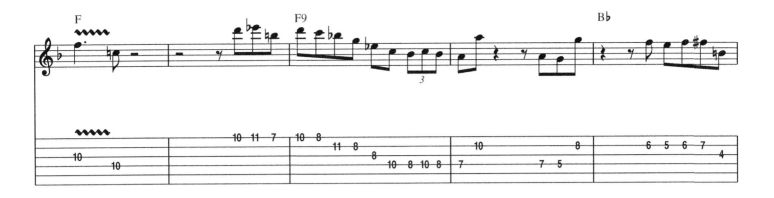

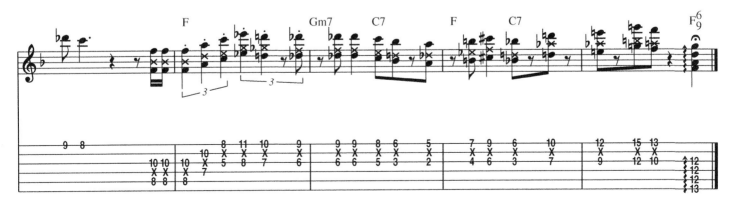

In a Mellow Tone

By Duke Ellington

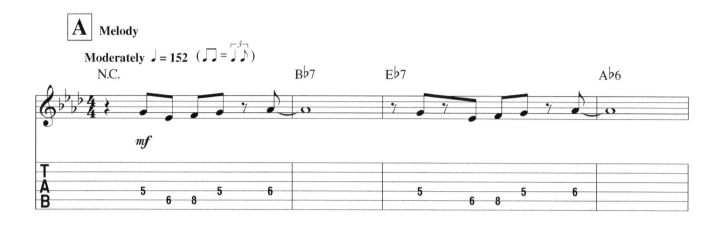

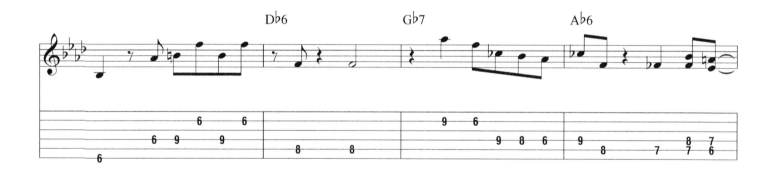

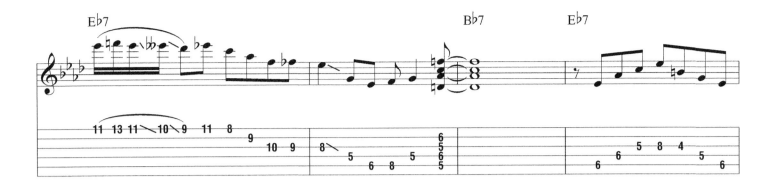

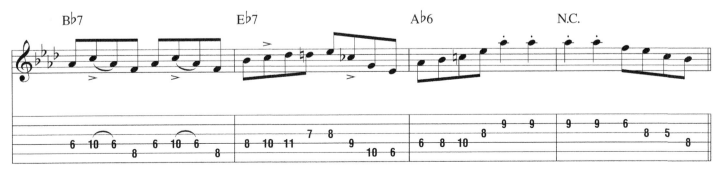

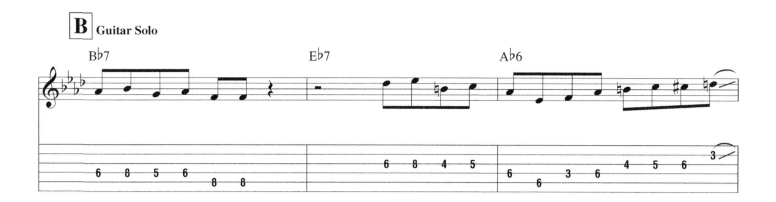

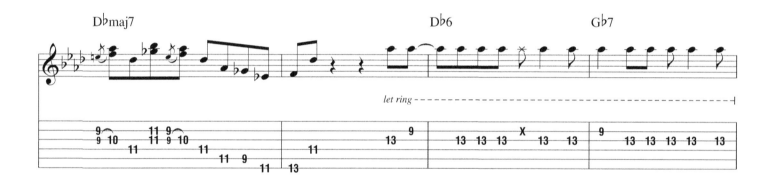

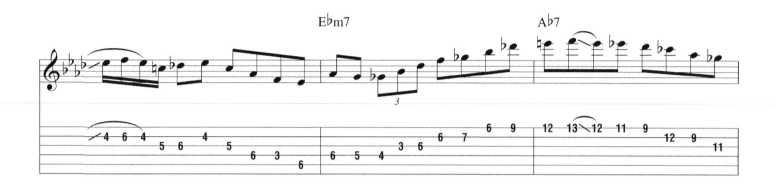

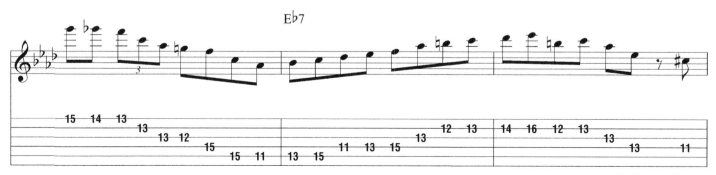

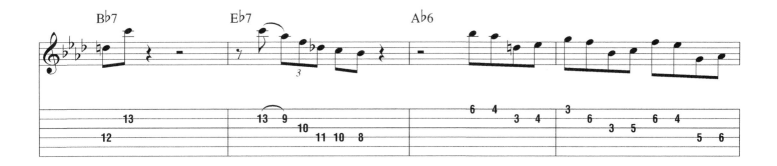

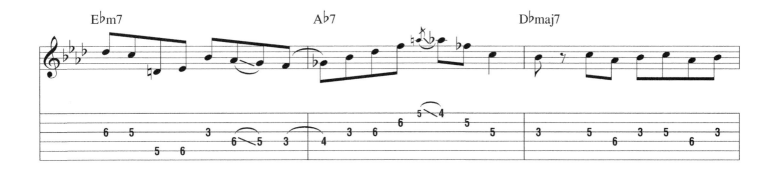

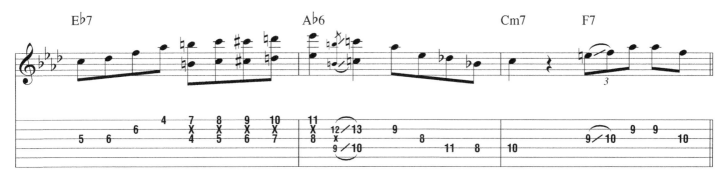

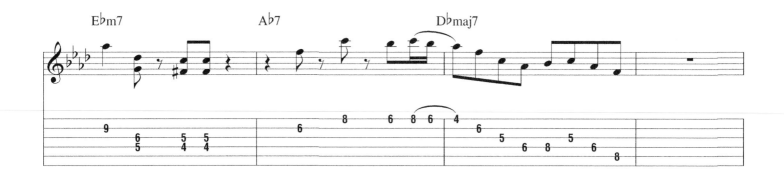

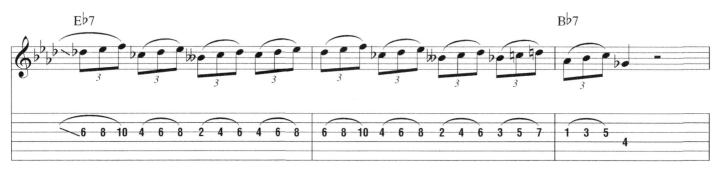

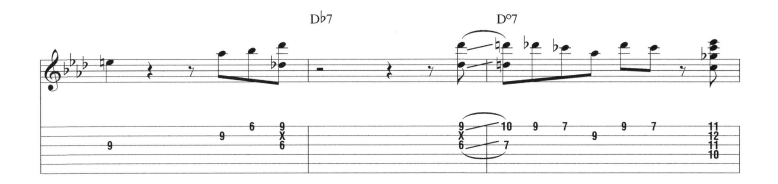

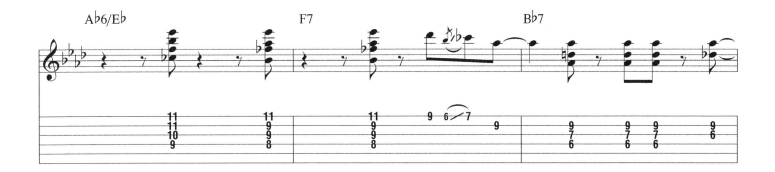

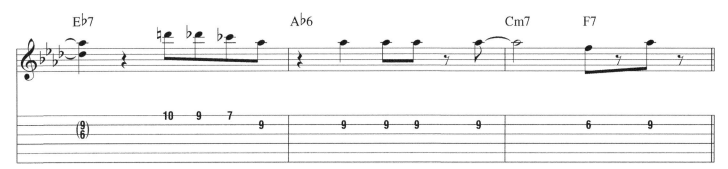

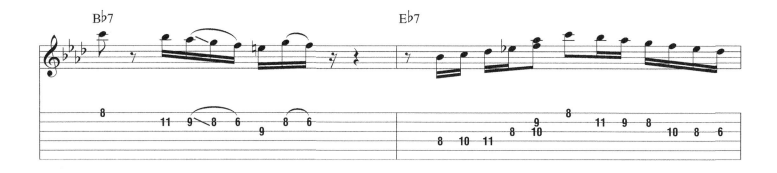

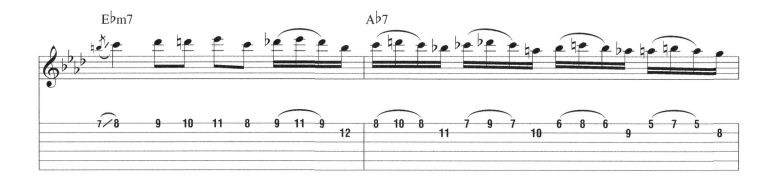

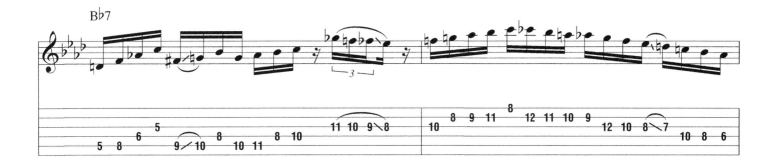

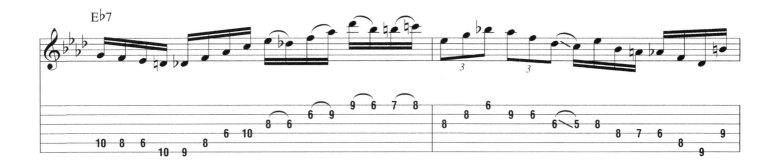

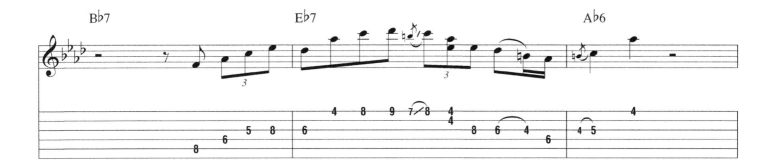

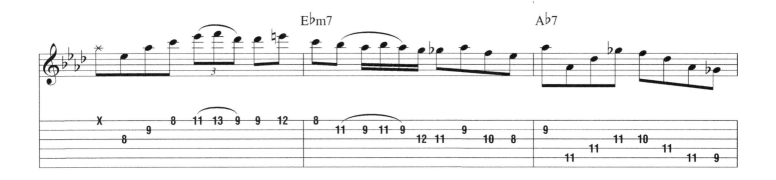

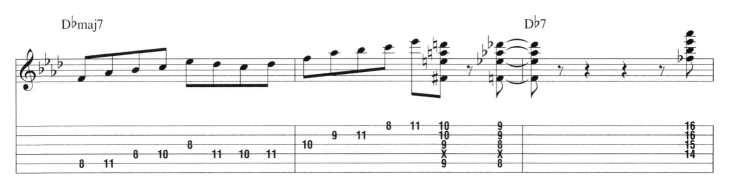

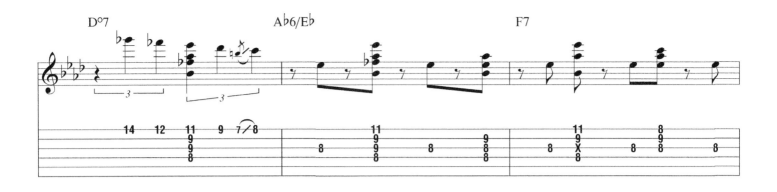

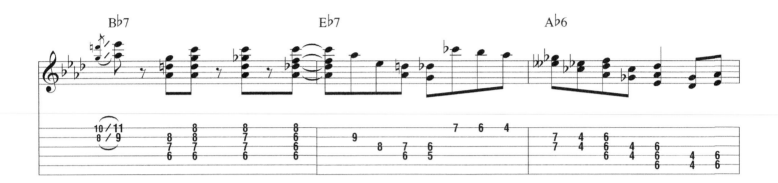

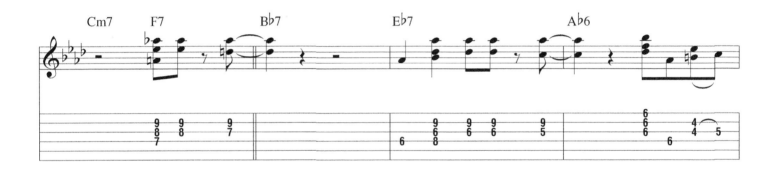

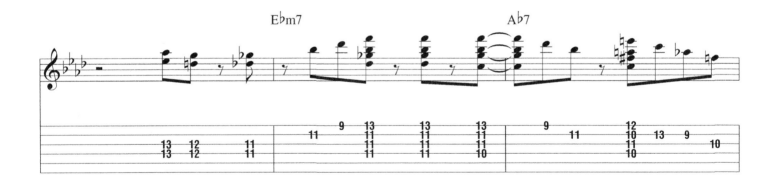

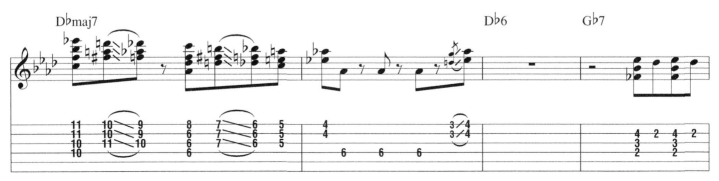

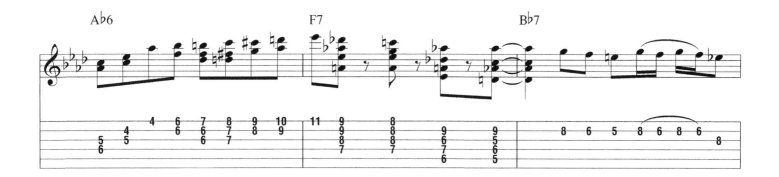

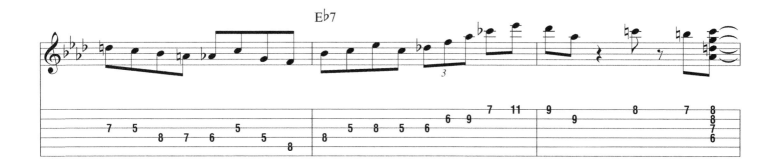

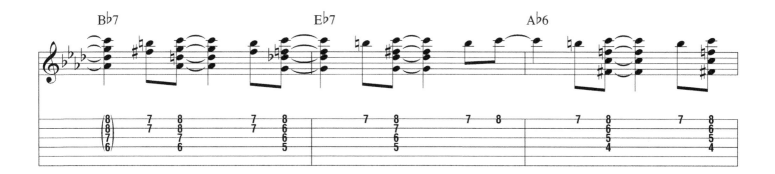

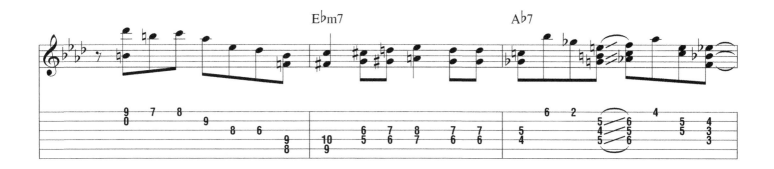

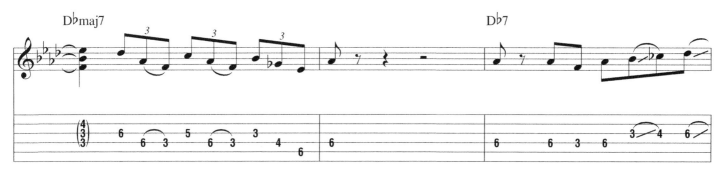

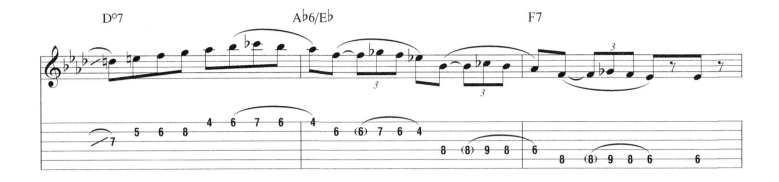

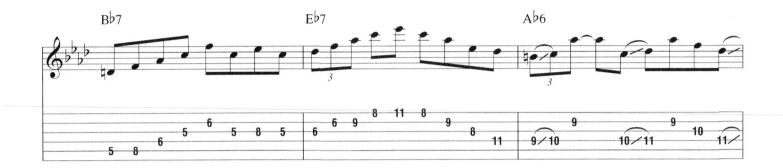

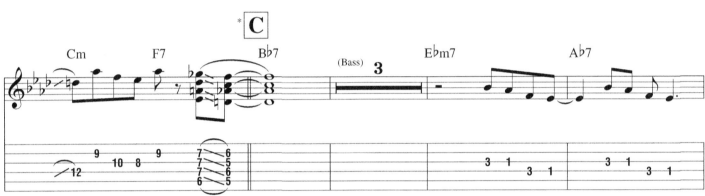

*Gtr. and bass exchange 4 meas. solos ("trade fours") throughout section.

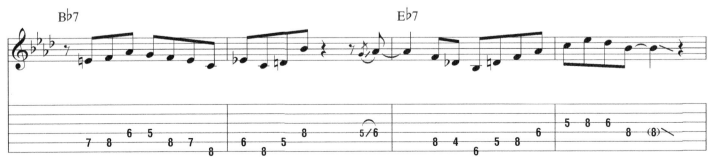

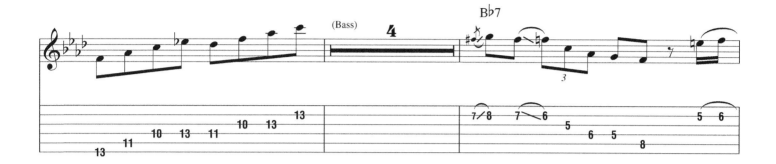

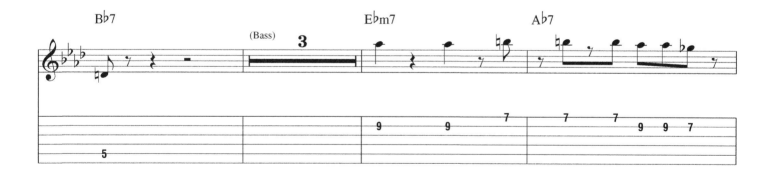

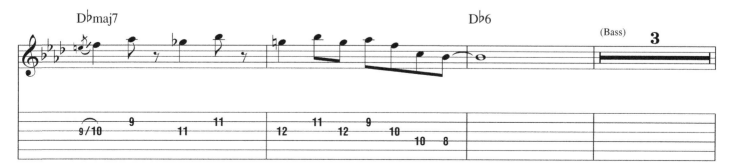

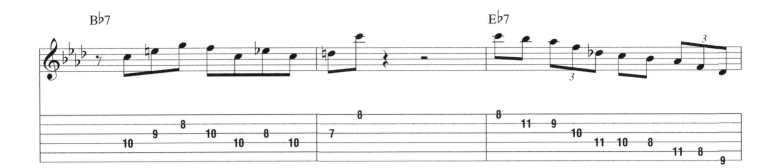

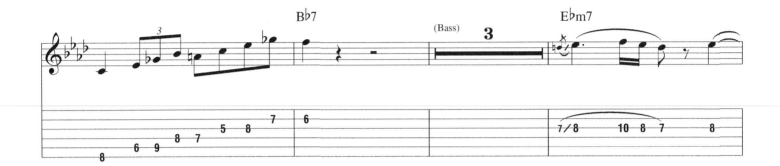

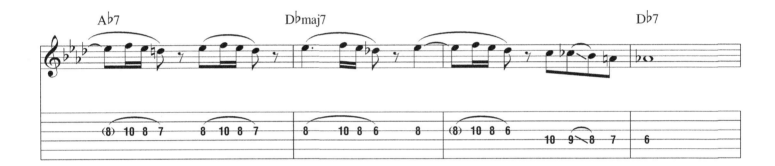

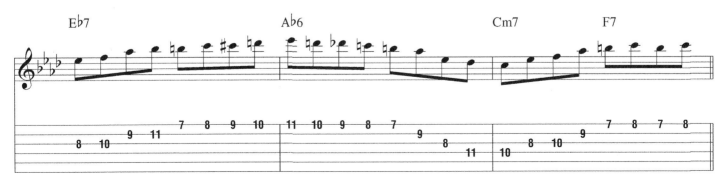

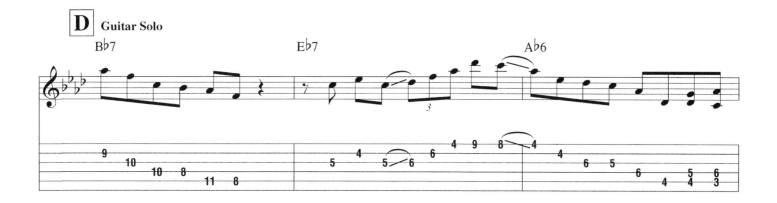

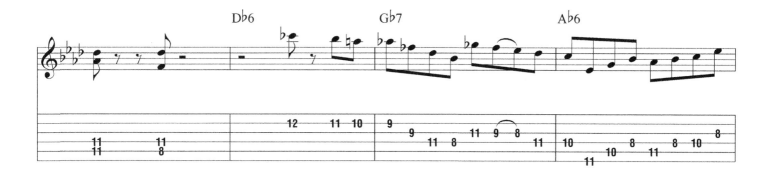

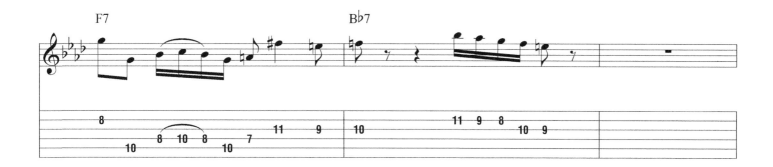

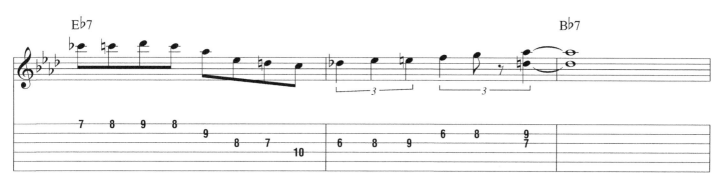

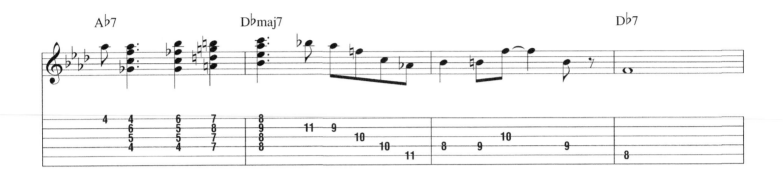

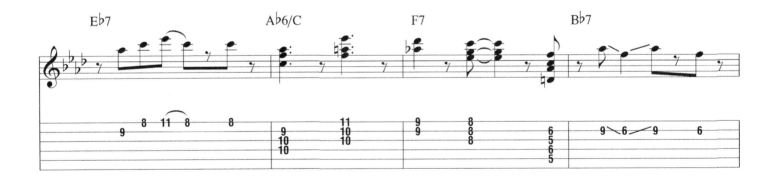

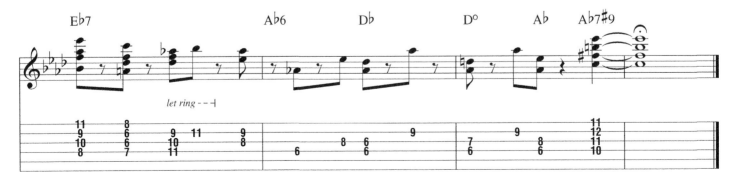

Things Ain't What They Used to Be

By Mercer Ellington

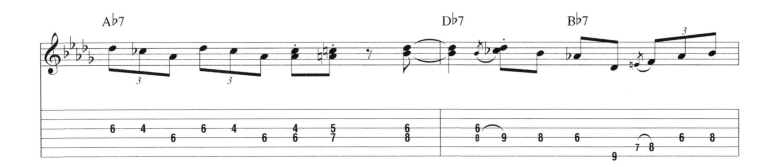

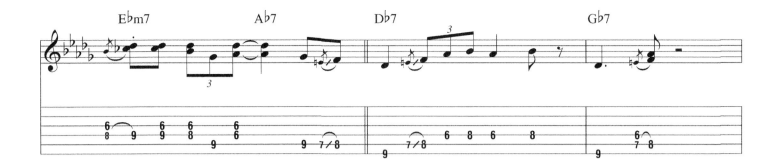

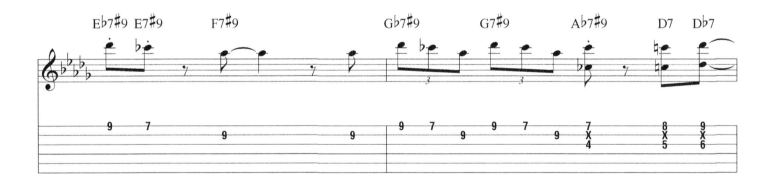

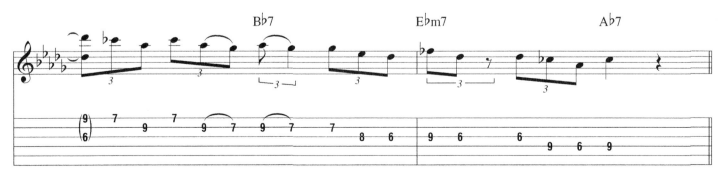

Guitar Solo

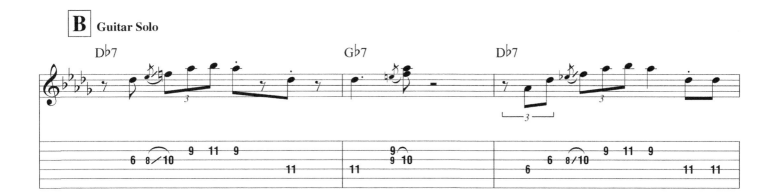

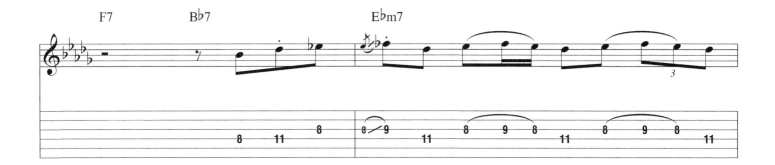

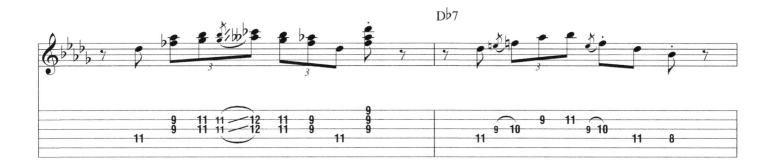

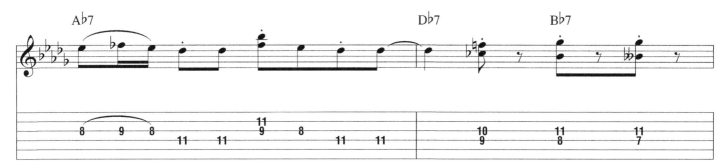

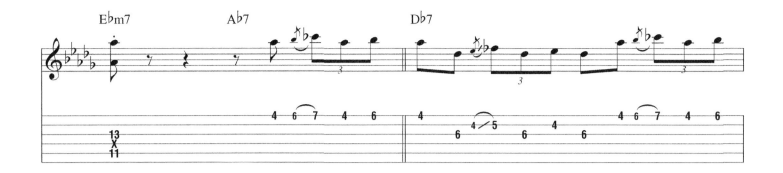

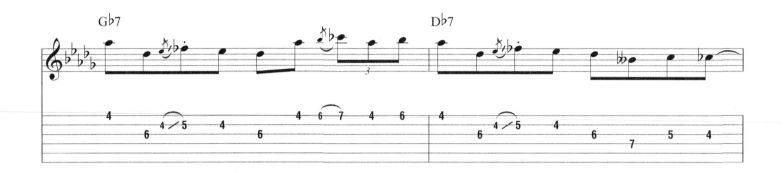

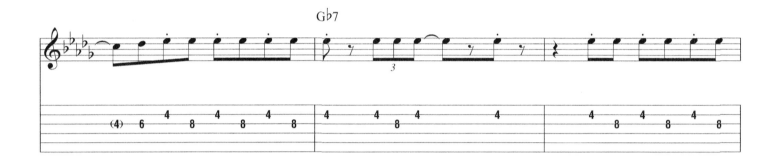

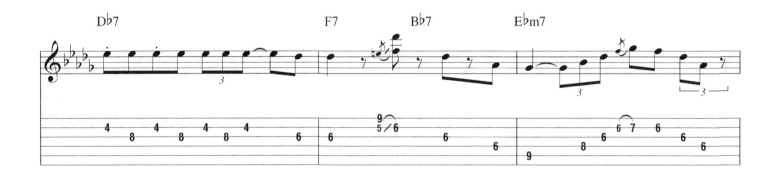

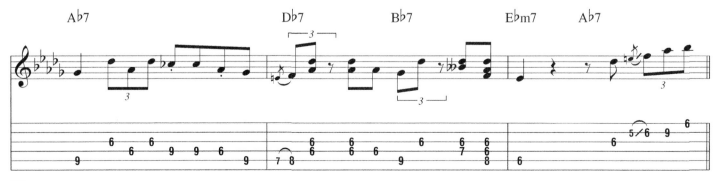

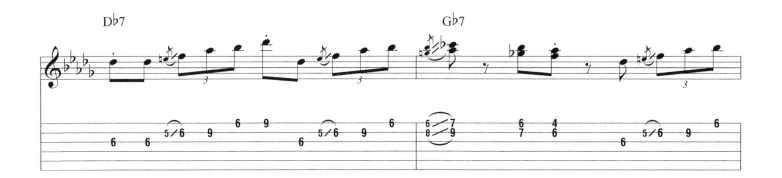

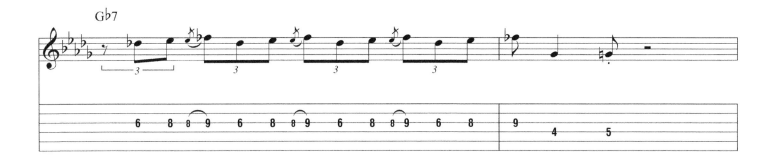

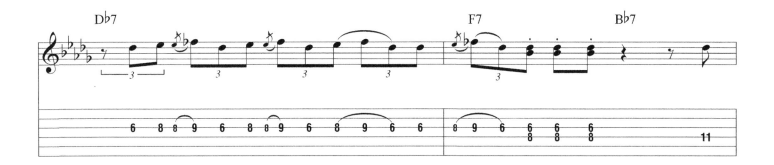

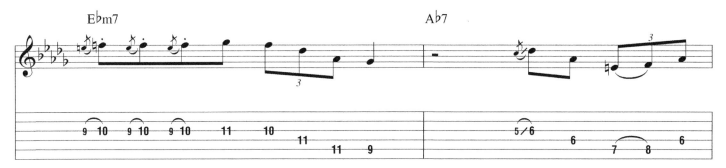

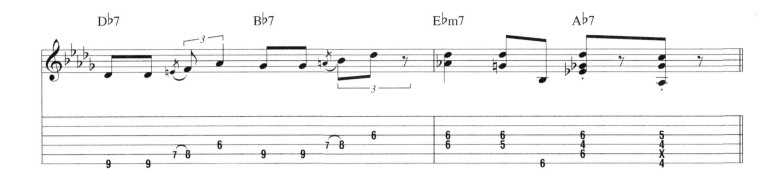

C Melody

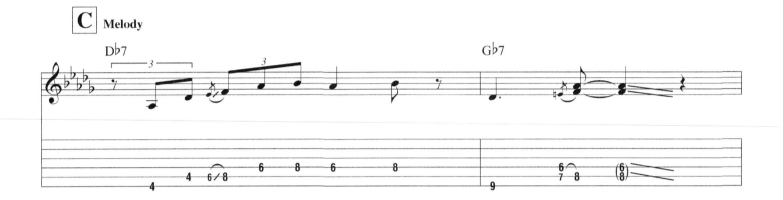

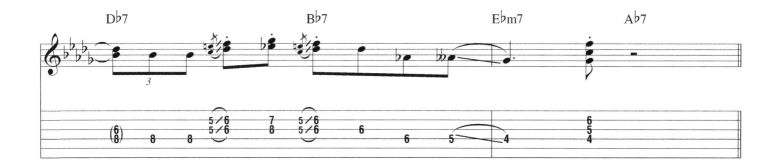

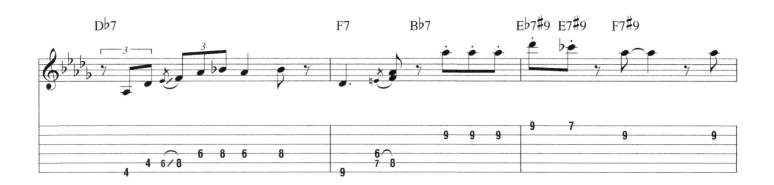

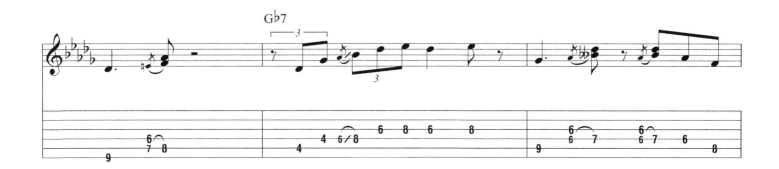

Moonlight in Vermont

Words by John Blackburn
Music by Karl Suessdorf

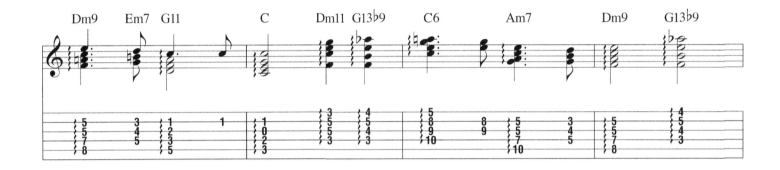

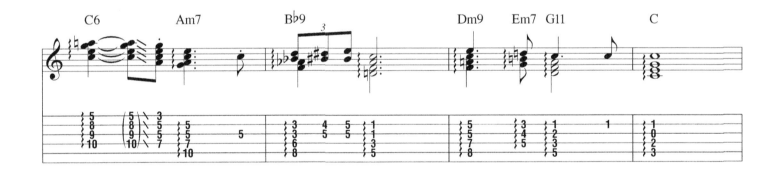

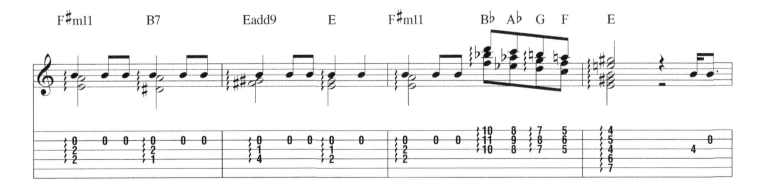

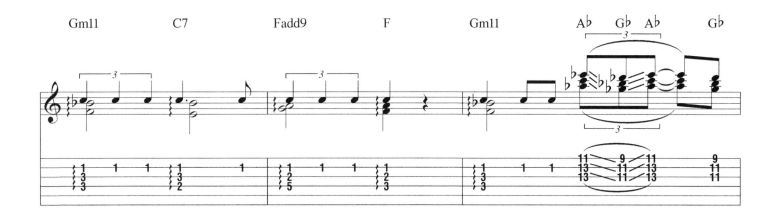

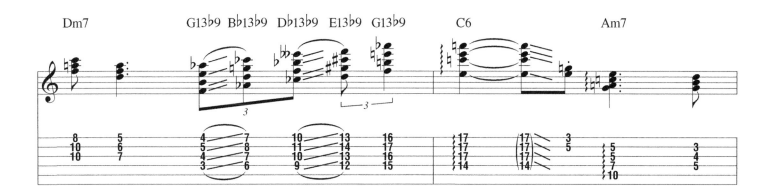

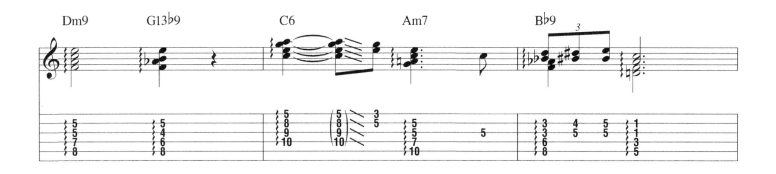

B Alto Sax Solo

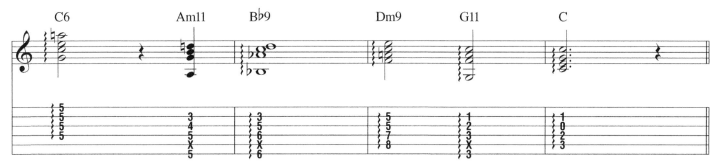

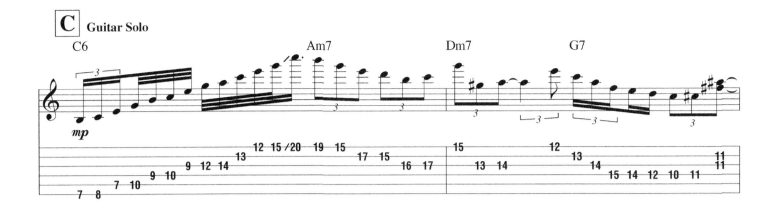

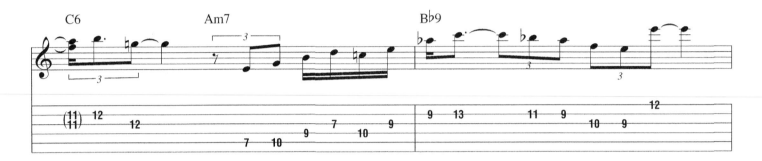

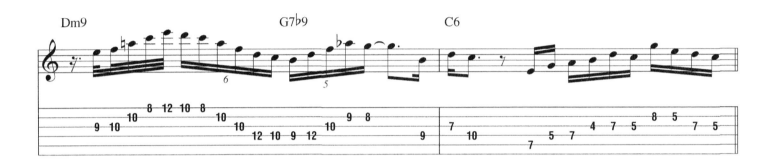

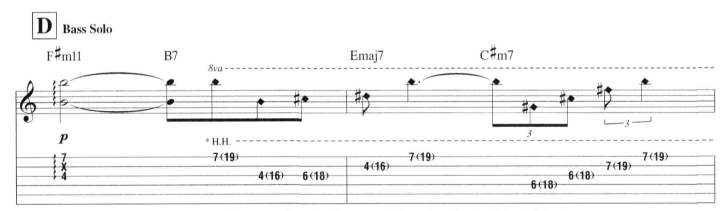

*Fret the note normally, and produce a harmonic by gently resting the pick hand's index finger directly above the indicated fret (in parentheses) while the pick hand's thumb or pick assists by plucking the appropriate string.

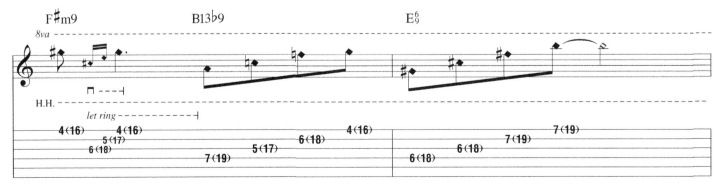

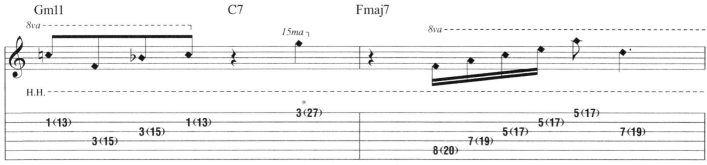

*Hypothetical fret location.

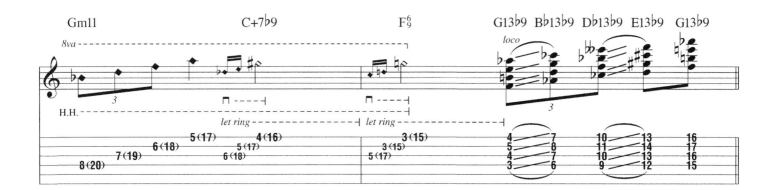

E Outro

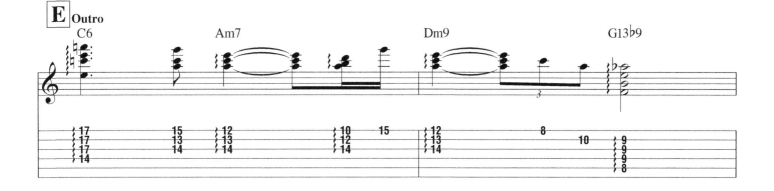

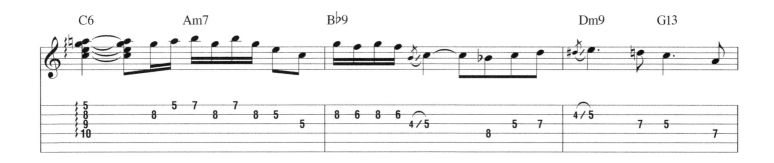

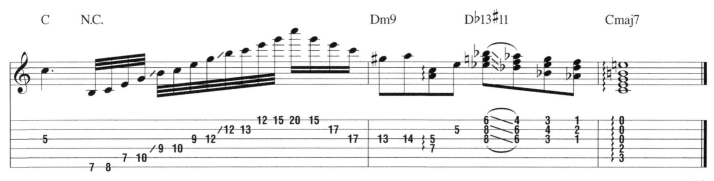

Satin Doll

from SOPHISTICATED LADIES
By Duke Ellington

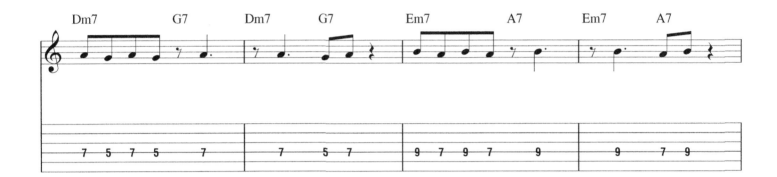

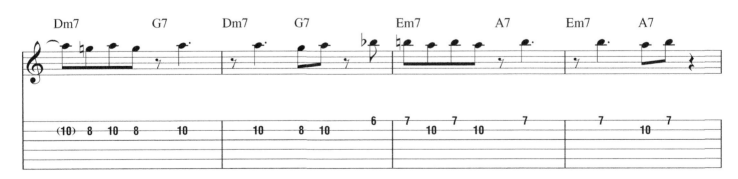

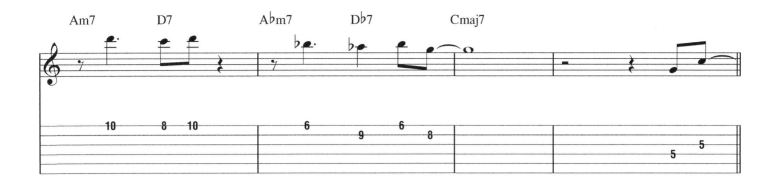

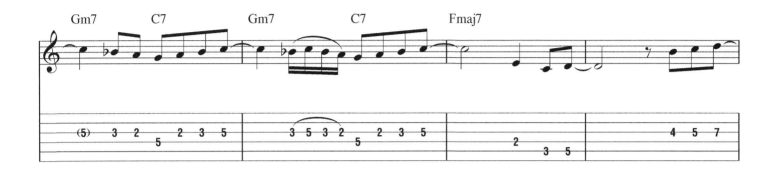

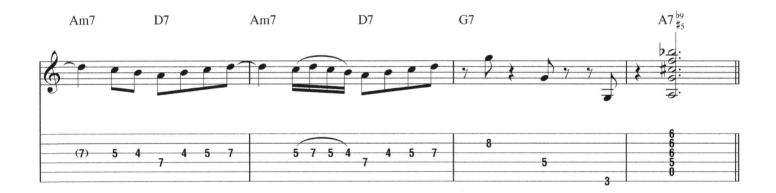

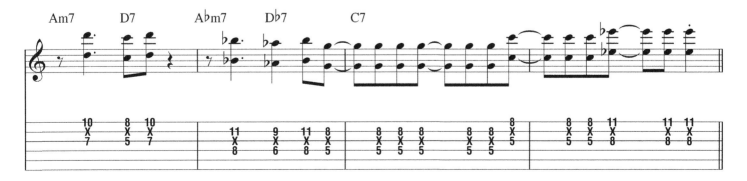

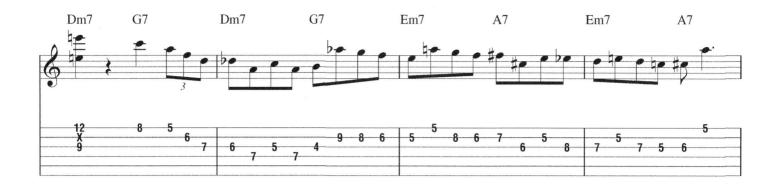

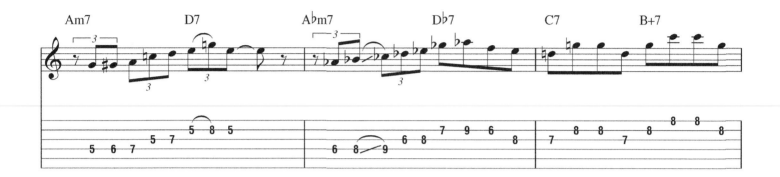

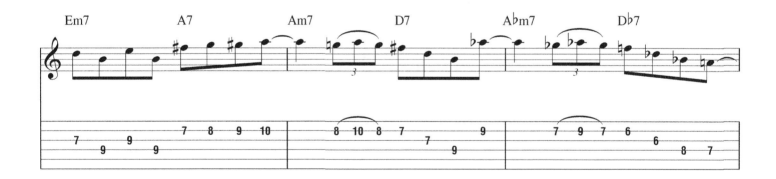

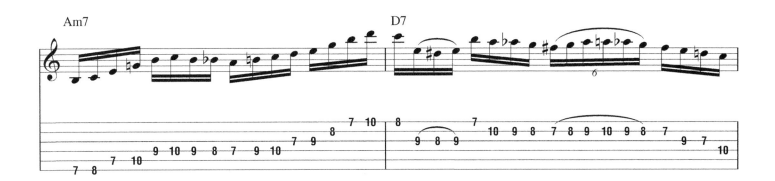

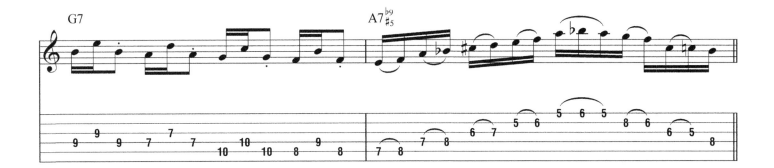

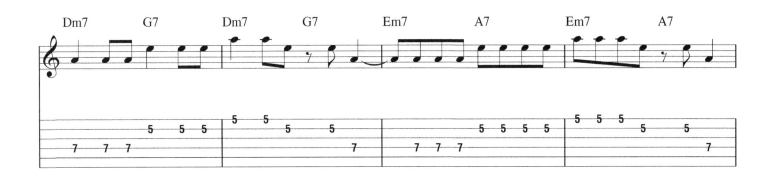

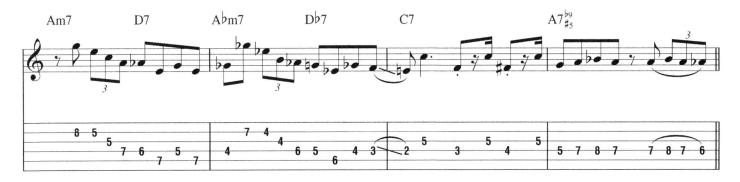

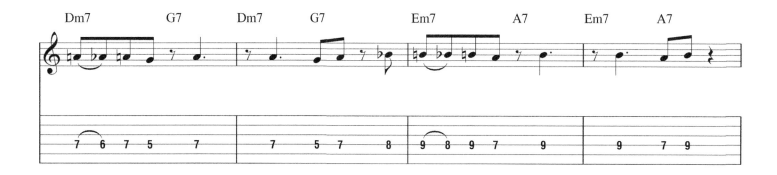

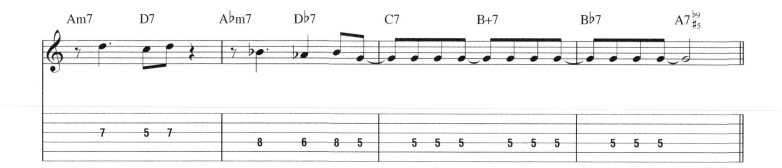

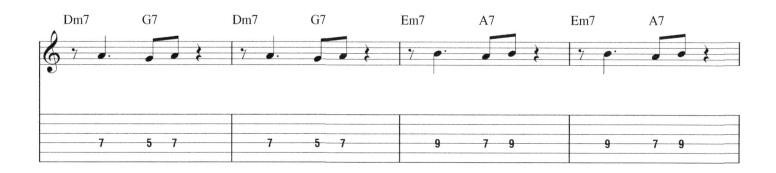

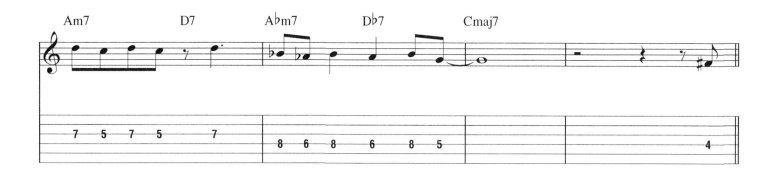

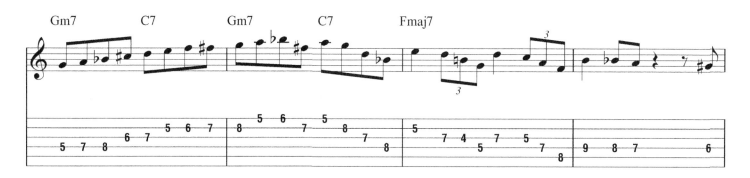

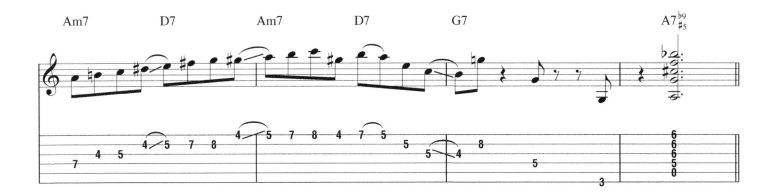

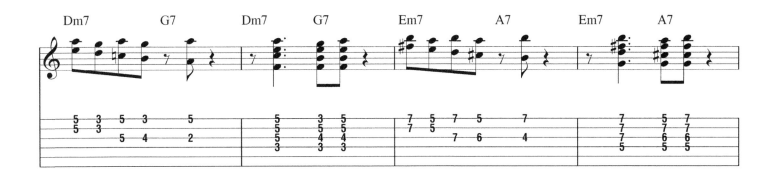

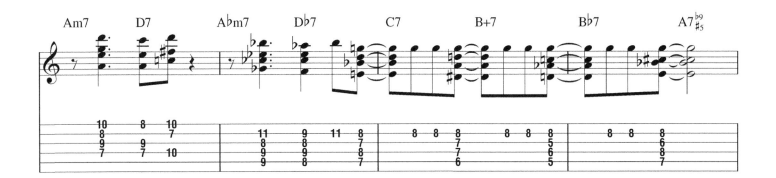

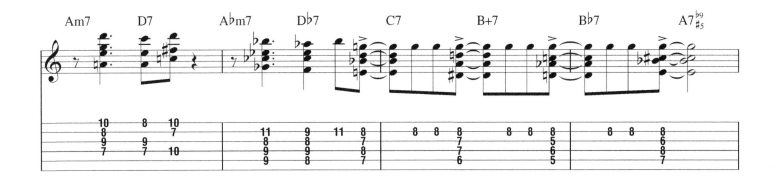

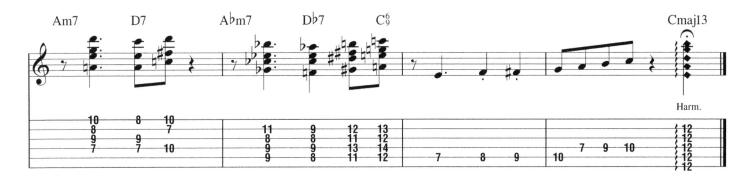

Speak Low

from the Musical Production ONE TOUCH OF VENUS

Words by Ogden Nash

Music by Kurt Weill

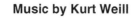

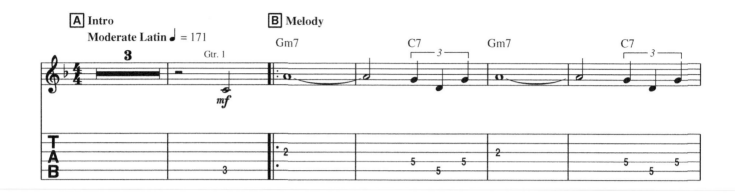

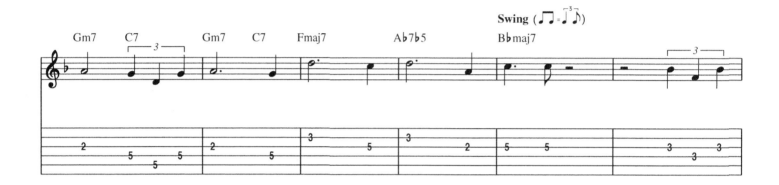

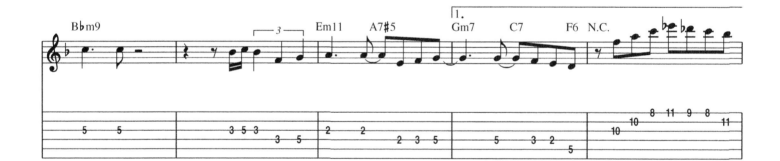

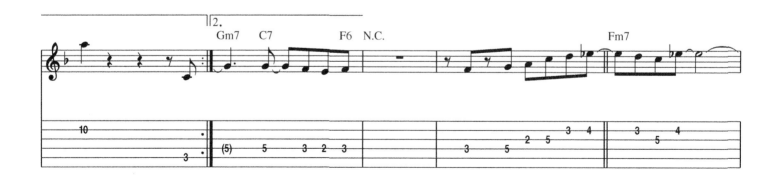

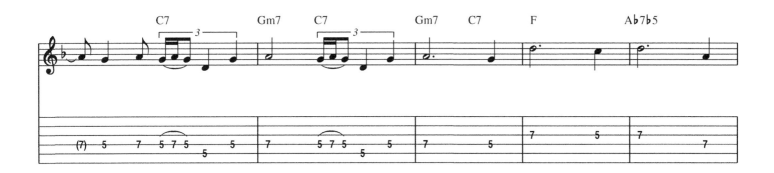

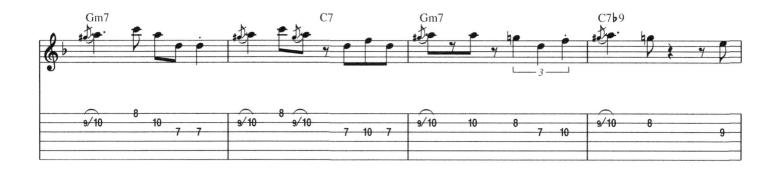

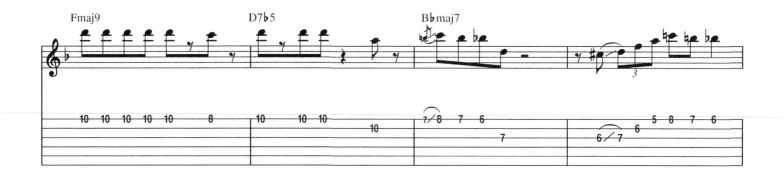

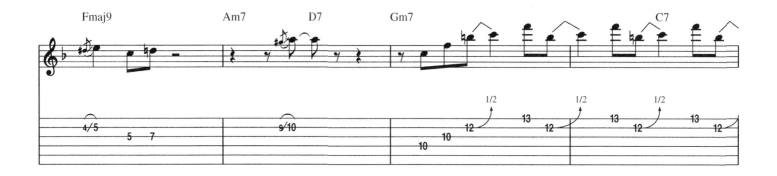

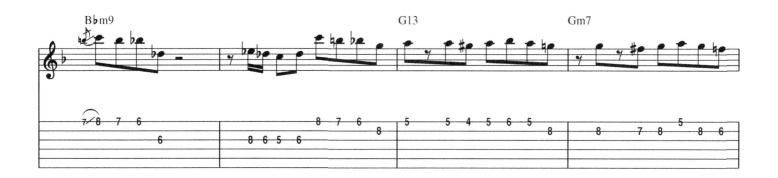

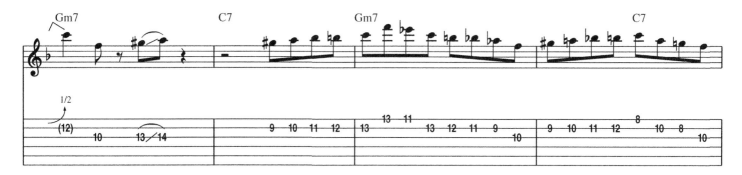

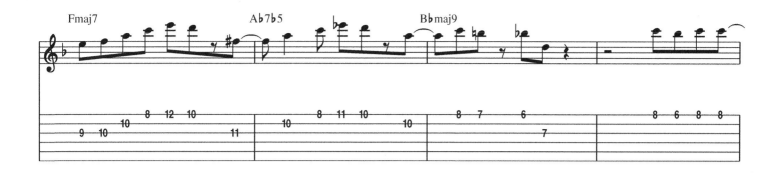

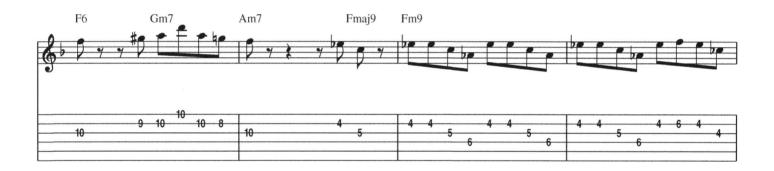

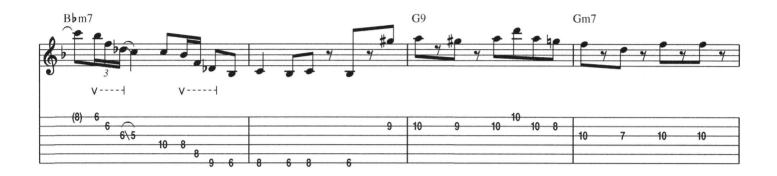

Guitar Notation Legend

THE MUSICAL STAFF shows pitches and rhythms and is divided by bar lines into measures. Pitches are named after the first seven letters of the alphabet.

TABLATURE graphically represents the guitar fingerboard. Each horizontal line represents a string, and each number represents a fret.

4th string, 2nd fret   1st & 2nd strings open, played together   open D chord

HALF-STEP BEND: Strike the note and bend up 1/2 step.

WHOLE-STEP BEND: Strike the note and bend up one step.

GRACE NOTE BEND: Strike the note and immediately bend up as indicated.

SLIGHT (MICROTONE) BEND: Strike the note and bend up 1/4 step.

BEND AND RELEASE: Strike the note and bend up as indicated, then release back to the original note. Only the first note is struck.

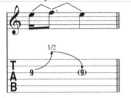

PRE-BEND: Bend the note as indicated, then strike it.

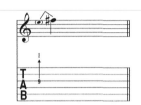

VIBRATO: The string is vibrated by rapidly bending and releasing the note with the fretting hand.

PALM MUTING: The note is partially muted by the pick hand lightly touching the string(s) just before the bridge.

HAMMER-ON: Strike the first (lower) note with one finger, then sound the higher note (on the same string) with another finger by fretting it without picking.

PULL-OFF: Place both fingers on the notes to be sounded. Strike the first note and without picking, pull the finger off to sound the second (lower) note.

LEGATO SLIDE: Strike the first note and then slide the same fret-hand finger up or down to the second note. The second note is not struck.

SHIFT SLIDE: Same as legato slide, except the second note is struck.

TRILL: Very rapidly alternate between the notes indicated by continuously hammering on and pulling off.

TAPPING: Hammer ("tap") the fret indicated with the pick-hand index or middle finger and pull off to the note fretted by the fret hand.

NATURAL HARMONIC: Strike the note while the fret-hand lightly touches the string directly over the fret indicated.

PINCH HARMONIC: The note is fretted normally and a harmonic is produced by adding the edge of the thumb or the tip of the index finger of the pick hand to the normal pick attack.

TREMOLO PICKING: The note is picked as rapidly and continuously as possible.

VIBRATO BAR DIVE AND RETURN: The pitch of the note or chord is dropped a specified number of steps (in rhythm), then returned to the original pitch.

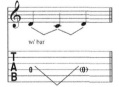

VIBRATO BAR SCOOP: Depress the bar just before striking the note, then quickly release the bar.

VIBRATO BAR DIP: Strike the note and then immediately drop a specified number of steps, then release back to the original pitch.

Additional Musical Definitions

(accent)   • Accentuate note (play it louder).

(staccato)   • Play the note short.

D.S. al Coda   • Go back to the sign (𝄋), then play until the measure marked *"To Coda,"* then skip to the section labelled **"Coda."**

D.C. al Fine   • Go back to the beginning of the song and play until the measure marked *"Fine"* (end).

Fill   • Label used to identify a brief melodic figure which is to be inserted into the arrangement.

N.C.   • Harmony is implied.

   • Repeat measures between signs.

• When a repeated section has different endings, play the first ending only the first time and the second ending only the second time.

HAL LEONARD GUITAR METHOD

METHOD BOOKS, SONGBOOKS AND REFERENCE BOOKS

THE HAL LEONARD GUITAR METHOD is designed for anyone just learning to play acoustic or electric guitar. It is based on years of teaching guitar students of all ages, and it also reflects some of the best guitar teaching ideas from around the world. This comprehensive method includes: A learning sequence carefully paced with clear instructions; popular songs which increase the incentive to learn to play; versatility – can be used as self-instruction or with a teacher; audio accompaniments so that students have fun and sound great while practicing.

BOOK 1
00699010 Book Only.............................$8.99
00699027 Book/Online Audio $12.99
00697341 Book/Online Audio + DVD $24.99
00697318 DVD Only $19.99
00155480 Deluxe Beginner Edition
(Book, CD, DVD, Online Audio/
Video & Chord Poster) $19.99

COMPLETE (BOOKS 1, 2 & 3)
00699040 Book Only...........................$16.99
00697342 Book/Online Audio $24.99

BOOK 2
00699020 Book Only.............................$8.99
00697313 Book/Online Audio $12.99

BOOK 3
00699030 Book Only.............................$8.99
00697316 Book/Online Audio $12.99

Prices, contents and availability subject to change without notice.

STYLISTIC METHODS

ACOUSTIC GUITAR
00697347 Method Book/Online Audio $17.99
00237969 Songbook/Online Audio $16.99

BLUEGRASS GUITAR
00697405 Method Book/Online Audio $16.99

BLUES GUITAR
00697326 Method Book/Online Audio (9" x 12") .$16.99
00697344 Method Book/Online Audio (6" x 9")...$15.99
00697385 Songbook/Online Audio (9" x 12")......$14.99
00248636 Kids Method Book/Online Audio $12.99

BRAZILIAN GUITAR
00697415 Method Book/Online Audio $17.99

CHRISTIAN GUITAR
00695947 Method Book/Online Audio $16.99
00697408 Songbook/CD Pack $14.99

CLASSICAL GUITAR
00697376 Method Book/Online Audio $15.99

COUNTRY GUITAR
00697337 Method Book/Online Audio $22.99
00697400 Songbook/Online Audio $19.99

FINGERSTYLE GUITAR
00697378 Method Book/Online Audio $21.99
00697432 Songbook/Online Audio $16.99

FLAMENCO GUITAR
00697363 Method Book/Online Audio $15.99

FOLK GUITAR
00697414 Method Book/Online Audio $16.99

JAZZ GUITAR
00695359 Book/Online Audio $22.99
00697386 Songbook/Online Audio $15.99

JAZZ-ROCK FUSION
00697387 Book/Online Audio $24.99

R&B GUITAR
00697356 Book/Online Audio $19.99
00697433 Songbook/CD Pack $14.99

ROCK GUITAR
00697319 Book/Online Audio $16.99
00697383 Songbook/Online Audio $16.99

ROCKABILLY GUITAR
00697407 Book/Online Audio $16.99

OTHER METHOD BOOKS

BARITONE GUITAR METHOD
00242055 Book/Online Audio $12.99

GUITAR FOR KIDS
00865003 Method Book 1/Online Audio $12.99
00697402 Songbook/Online Audio $9.99
00128437 Method Book 2/Online Audio $12.99

MUSIC THEORY FOR GUITARISTS
00695790 Book/Online Audio $19.99

TENOR GUITAR METHOD
00148330 Book/Online Audio $12.99

12-STRING GUITAR METHOD
00249528 Book/Online Audio $19.99

METHOD SUPPLEMENTS

ARPEGGIO FINDER
00697352 6" x 9" Edition $6.99
00697351 9" x 12" Edition $9.99

BARRE CHORDS
00697406 Book/Online Audio $14.99

CHORD, SCALE & ARPEGGIO FINDER
00697410 Book Only..$19.99

GUITAR TECHNIQUES
00697389 Book/Online Audio $16.99

INCREDIBLE CHORD FINDER
00697200 6" x 9" Edition $7.99
00697208 9" x 12" Edition $7.99

INCREDIBLE SCALE FINDER
00695568 6" x 9" Edition $9.99
00695490 9" x 12" Edition $9.99

LEAD LICKS
00697345 Book/Online Audio $10.99

RHYTHM RIFFS
00697346 Book/Online Audio $14.99

SONGBOOKS

CLASSICAL GUITAR PIECES
00697388 Book/Online Audio $9.99

EASY POP MELODIES
00697281 Book Only..$7.99
00697440 Book/Online Audio $14.99

(MORE) EASY POP MELODIES
00697280 Book Only..$6.99
00697269 Book/Online Audio $14.99

(EVEN MORE) EASY POP MELODIES
00699154 Book Only..$6.99
00697439 Book/Online Audio $14.99

EASY POP RHYTHMS
00697336 Book Only..$7.99
00697441 Book/Online Audio $14.99

(MORE) EASY POP RHYTHMS
00697338 Book Only..$7.99
00697322 Book/Online Audio $14.99

(EVEN MORE) EASY POP RHYTHMS
00697340 Book Only..$7.99
00697323 Book/Online Audio $14.99

EASY POP CHRISTMAS MELODIES
00697417 Book Only..$9.99
00697416 Book/Online Audio $14.99

EASY POP CHRISTMAS RHYTHMS
00278177 Book Only..$6.99
00278175 Book/Online Audio $14.99

EASY SOLO GUITAR PIECES
00110407 Book Only..$9.99

REFERENCE

GUITAR PRACTICE PLANNER
00697401 Book Only..$5.99

GUITAR SETUP & MAINTENANCE
00697427 6" x 9" Edition $14.99
00697421 9" x 12" Edition $12.99

For more info, songlists, or to purchase these and more books from your favorite music retailer, go to

halleonard.com

HAL•LEONARD®

HAL•LEONARD® GUITAR PLAY-ALONG

This series will help you play your favorite songs quickly and easily. Just follow the tab and listen to the audio to the hear how the guitar should sound, and then play along using the separate backing tracks. Audio files also include software to slow down the tempo without changing pitch. The melody and lyrics are included in the book so that you can sing or simply follow along.

INCLUDES TAB

Complete song lists available online.

Prices, contents, and availability subject to change without notice.

www.halleonard.com

0820
173